To Graydon & Diane

Thank you for y
appreciate your friendship
years. You guys have been so
incredibly encouraging. It is an
honor to be called your friend.
Keep making lemonade!

God Bless,
David Bidger
(Mark McKring)

When Life Hands You Lemons …

Inspiring Stories of Tenacious Teens

DAVID BRIDGES

WestBow·
PRESS
A DIVISION OF THOMAS NELSON
& ZONDERVAN

WestBow Press books may be ordered through booksellers or by contacting:

WestBow Press
A Division of Thomas Nelson & Zondervan
1663 Liberty Drive
Bloomington, IN 47403
www.westbowpress.com
1 (866) 928-1240

ISBN: 978-1-4908-3367-5 (sc)
ISBN: 978-1-4908-3366-8 (hc)
ISBN: 978-1-4908-3368-2 (e)

Library of Congress Control Number: 2014906599

Printed in the United States of America.

WestBow Press rev. date: 04/24/2014

CONTENTS

This work is a memoir. It reflects the author's present recollection of experiences over a period of years and may not coincide with what others depicted in the story experienced or remember. Therefore, in consideration of that fact and in the interest of protecting identities and privacy, I have changed relationships, names, cities, states, and other identifiable information.

ACKNOWLEDGMENTS

This very well could be the most difficult section to write in the entire book. I am eager to all those who made the endeavor possible, but I am also fearful of forgetting someone who deserves to be mentioned here. With that in mind, I apologize in advance to anyone I failed to thank.

I would be remiss to start anywhere other than my beautiful wife of thirty years. Robbin, your constant encouragement, support, and patience mean the world to me. I will be forever grateful for the personal sacrifices you made that inspired me to finish this project. Thank you for saying, "I do," back in '83. Thank you for fulfilling that promise every day since then. I love you—always have and always will.

To my three daughters, Shannon, Rhema, and Amy, I want to say thanks. Shannon and Rhema, thank you so much for your editing help and feedback along the way. I know it is hard to give constructive feedback to your dad (although Rhema could have made it seem more difficult). Amy, thank you for understanding the hours at the computer that could have been spent with you. You know how much I wish I was there for you more. And then there is Trevor. Thank you for your friendship, but especially for how well you love my daughter. In my heart, I threw out the "in-law" part of your title a long time ago.

I would also like to acknowledge Hank Sword of Market Impact for the incredible cover. If the book can live up to title, it should be a great success! I want to also thank Tim Sawtelle for help with the website www.4bigrocks.com. Your expertise was greatly appreciated.

Your patience with my techno-illiteracy was phenomenal. To Nancy Smith, thank you for your friendship as well as your insight and wisdom along the way.

I am so grateful to all my friends and family who supported me through your encouraging words and your prayers. I am grateful to the Grays and Gurleys—you know how I feel about you—and to all my friends and "family" who were a part of CF. You will forever be in my heart.

I also want say how grateful I am to work with so many wonderful teachers, coaches, and administrators over the past decade. It has been quite a journey. I consider it an honor and privilege not only to work alongside you but also to call you my friends.

To all my kids, both at home and at school.
You have enriched my life more than you will ever know.

FOREWORD

Several years ago, I was working with kids that were struggling in school and in their, oftentimes, difficult situations at home...if they had one. It was during that time that I wrote the curriculum for Teen Leadership. Little did I know that it would spread nationwide and into India and other countries. Today, well over 2,000,000 young people have gone through the program, most for course credit in their high schools.

I wrote the curriculum and taught the course in the beginning but soon came to realize that my efforts were not even remotely going to make the transformation possible for young people that I wanted to see.

Teachers began to ask if they could teach the course in their high schools and middle schools. School boards wanted the curriculum because of the research behind the processes and the dramatic drop in discipline referrals and truancy.

That's when we met David Bridges. He was one of those guys who connected with kids but he was not an educator. When he asked us what he needed to do to teach these processes and course to young people, we simply said, "Become a teacher and make a difference in the lives of the kids and their schools." I cannot tell you how many times we had said that to people and they get that far away look and ask if there is another way to do it. Teachers teach. Great teachers transform!

David left his profession, went back to school and became a teacher. His family made sacrifices and he spent long hours so he could become a teacher.

But, that's not really what David Bridges did. He became a life giver.

This book is about life...the tragedies and the victories; the challenges and the opportunities. I cried over some of the kids' stories and couldn't help but reread several of them....the kids whose stories are shared here are amazing and you will be challenged and better for knowing these young people.

These kids are incredible and their teacher is the difference.

Flip Flippen
Chairman, The Flippen Group
New York Times Best-selling Author of *The Flip Side*

INTRODUCTION

It was a cool, sunny March afternoon in Mississippi. I was having a working lunch with James, the assistant superintendent of my school district. We were both serving on a district committee, so we decided to discuss some pressing issues over a working lunch. James chaired the committee.

I always had a great deal of respect for James. He had served the district for many years as a teacher, coach, and later principal at one of the local elementary schools. He had been serving as assistant superintendent for a couple of years at the time of our lunch. After discussing the business at hand, James asked how my classes were going. That is one of my all-time favorite questions. There are very few things I get more passionate about discussing than my students. James asked what time it was. Little did he know I was determined to build him a watch.

"James, you know I teach a speech class called Teen Leadership, right?"

"Yes, I knew that," replied James.

"Well, next week I will be taking six of my Teen Leadership students to give speeches at a Capturing Kids' Hearts (CKH) conference." I went on to tell him this would be my nineteenth CKH and that I had brought more than one hundred students to give speeches at these events over the past five years.

James's facial expression spoke volumes. The news was exciting for him to hear but was also quite puzzling. "I didn't know you had ever taken students to a Capturing Kids' Hearts conference."

I have to admit that I had mixed feelings about James's response. It was sad to learn that an administrator from our district was unaware I had taken *any* students to these conferences. Of course, it was not his fault. I did not go out of my way to tell everyone about our conferences and how the lives of both the teachers and my students were changed for the better. But James's response also confirmed that I needed to write about our experiences both at the CKH conferences as well as our classroom. The students' stories were just too inspirational to keep them to ourselves.

At this point, the reader may be asking, "What is a Capturing Kids' Hearts conference and a Teen Leadership class, anyway?" I am glad you asked. The Flippen Group is one of the leading trainers of teachers in the United States. This company and its founder, Flip Flippen, created both the CKH conferences as well as the curriculum for the Teen Leadership class I teach.

Teen Leadership is a speech class that teaches students leadership, business, and professional skills. We teach students important lessons concerning the character, qualities, and skills an effective leader possesses. We teach our students not only how to be successful business professionals when they become adults but how to be successful *people*. We not only teach them how to have a successful career but also how to have a successful marriage and family. We emphasize the importance of first impressions, integrity, hard work, and respect for those with whom we work. I heard a wise man once say, "Some things are better caught than taught." So one way we teach the students how to have healthy family relationships is by building a family, or team atmosphere, in our classroom. On the last day of our class, it is not uncommon at all to pass around the box of tissues we always have handy. We really become "family" in many ways.

A Capturing Kids' Hearts (CKH) conference is a three-day conference for teachers of all subject areas and all grade levels. The premise behind this conference is this: "If you don't have a kid's heart, you will never have his mind." CKH not only gives teachers strategies in how to capture the hearts of their students, but it also teaches them that capturing a kid's heart is more of a process and lifestyle than a program that they try to implement until the next fad comes along.

What makes CKH unique is that at the end of the second day of their flagship CKH conferences, the Flippen Group invites a Teen Leadership teacher to bring up to six students to give three- to five-minute speeches about how Teen Leadership has changed their lives, since Teen Leadership epitomizes the Capturing Kids' Hearts philosophy. It is one thing to hear trainers at a conference demonstrate the value of the information they are sharing; it is quite another for teachers to have six students (thirteen- and fourteen-year-olds) stand up, look them in the eye, and tell them how the CKH process has changed their lives. When I was thirteen I would not enter a room with fifty teachers, much less give a speech in front of them. Many *teachers* today would be afraid to speak to fifty teachers!

I was seriously deliberating whether or not I should write this book after talking with James. So in March 2010, I escorted six of my students to a CKH conference and the students spoke with such confidence and grace that the teachers were astonished. After the students' speeches, I spoke to the teachers about how the process has changed my teaching career. Following the speeches, we retired to the dining hall, where the students and I sat at separate tables so we could visit with the teachers over dinner.

There were four teachers at my table, and I began to answer questions that inevitably come up. Then I began to tell them stories of other students who were unable to attend. After only a few minutes, I noticed that tears filled the eyes of all four teachers at my table. That is when I knew our story had to be told. One of the teachers later wrote me an encouraging note and said she could have listened to me forever. Though I will try not to make this book last forever, I challenge you enter the lives of these students and embrace the emotion of their stories. I intentionally wrote this book to be an "easy read," because "busy" does not begin to describe the lives of most parents and teachers. And besides, the readers of this book need time to make stories of their own.

Each semester in my class, I show the movie *Freedom Writers*. It is the story of the incredible impact a teacher named Ms. Erin Gruwell made on her students in a high school in Long Beach, California. Many of her students were economically disadvantaged and were involved in gang activity. Yet through her perseverance and the love she shared with her students, their lives were changed. At the dinner with these teachers, I told them, as I have told others hundreds of times, we have several *"Freedom Writers* moments" in my class every semester. Well, to be honest, I am tired of saying that, because the moments we have shared together are not *"Freedom Writers* moments." They are our moments. It is our story.

The Power of "Story"

Author John Eldridge *(Journey of Desire, Wild at Heart, Waking the Dead),* wrote, "Story is the language of the heart." There is a reason when our parents tucked us in bed at night they read us bedtime *stories* and not the bedtime financial statements. Logic and cognitive information may educate and enrich the mind but will do little to capture the heart. In this book, we will share with you strategies, concepts, and even techniques that will allow you reach your full "relational" potential. Whether you are relating to students, your children, your spouse, or your coworkers, this book is for you. Yet without the stories, this book would be just one of an infinite number of how-to books that collect dust on shelves in libraries, bookstores, and bedrooms across America. The stories of these students will renew your confidence in today's youth, strengthen your own resolve and courage, and hopefully motivate you to make a difference in the lives of those with whom you have influence today.

You will read about stories of great turmoil and struggle; hopelessness and pain; courage and resolve; choices to be made and prices to be paid. I warn you, some of the stories will be difficult to read. They were difficult to write. Many of these students have been abused, neglected, and written off by their parents. Some sat by helplessly as they have witnessed their fathers being arrested. Some have discovered the lifeless body of a parent shortly after the parent had committed suicide. Others were told by their fathers or mothers that they were a mistake, or an accident, and should never have been born. Many have tried to cope with parents who were drug addicts and alcoholics, and some have shared in these struggles themselves. Yet the courage and determination they have demonstrated in overcoming these obstacles in life are nothing short of miraculous.

Yes, there have been conflicts. But how many great stories have you read without conflict? The conflict is what makes the story. The hero or heroine overcoming the conflict is what inspires us to overcome the struggles in our own lives! No one should have to endure what these kids have been through at such a young age. Yet their hope and perseverance continue to amaze me.

My hope and prayer is that this book will inspire all who read it, whether they are in education or not. The stories took place in the context of an educational setting, but the stories are universal and will translate into any culture, career, or family. The stories are real because the people are real. Prepare yourself to laugh, cry, and simply be inspired by the stories of these amazing young people. They have indelibly left a mark on my life, and I hope they will do the same for you as you read their stories.

When Life Hands You Lemons ...

There was a famous saying in the '70s (yes, I am dating myself) found on numerous bumper stickers and posters. It went something like this: "When life hands you lemons, make lemonade." This book is about students who have been handed lemons in life. Rather than allowing these lemons to make them sour, they have chosen not only to make lemonade for themselves but to build lemonade stands so that others can taste how wonderful their lemonade tastes.

As you read these stories, my hope is that you will recognize the God-given dreams, passions, and talents that lie deep inside of you. It is only when we tap into these dreams and live fully from our heart that we will see our world changed.

Later in this book, we will discuss life lessons that translate far beyond the educational realm. These lessons will empower the reader to cast off the restraints that keep us from being all we were meant to be. The stories you will read in this book would be nonexistent if I had done only what was asked of me as a teacher. There would be no stories without the students' willingness to change. These stories would not have been without dreams—the dreams of some inspirational kids and a white-haired old man. Remember this: if your dreams do not scare you, you are not dreaming big enough.

I am periodically asked a very intriguing question: "What do you want written on your tombstone?" The answer is easy. "He didn't play it safe." May these stories inspire you to make stories of your own.

Chapter 1

FRESH-SQUEEZED, ANYONE?

My favorite family holiday dish is my wife's lemon pie. The word *delicious* does not do it justice. Her recipe calls for two cups of fresh-squeezed lemon juice. So one Thanksgiving, when my wife, Robbin, asked me if I could squeeze the lemons for the pie, I was more than happy to assist. Anything that would hasten the process of creating the best lemon pie in the world was fine by me.

As I squeezed the lemons and meditated on the luscious goodness of lemon juice gently falling into the waiting arms of the mixing bowl, I had a random thought. Why was the lemon juice sour? Was it because of pressure it was under? Or could it be sour just because it was inside the lemon?

The pressure I was applying to the lemon had nothing to do with making the lemon juice sour. All the pressure did was force what was once inside the lemon to come out. Most of us face pressures of various degrees on a weekly, if not daily, basis. It is as though we are the stars of our very own soap operas. In the average soap opera, we find the star in, about to get in, or just getting out of … trouble. The pressures we face are simply tools used to force whatever is inside of us to come out. If pressures cause us to become angry, it is because there was already anger in our heart. If we allow ourselves to use the pressures of life as an excuse to quit, it is because we were already looking for an excuse to quit.

This book is titled *When Life Hands You Lemons …* because it is filled with stories of inspiring kids who have faced the toughest battles life has to offer. Yet they have not used these setbacks as excuses, nor have they allowed these challenges to strip them of their hope. Rather than stumbling into the pit of despair, they have used these challenges as footholds to reach great heights. Many adults say, "These kids today!" as they throw up their hands in resignation. I say, "These kids today!" while I throw up my hands to high-five them. It is said that children are our future. If our future depends on kids like those you will read about in this book, we are in good hands.

"I could never do what you do," Bobby said.

"What are you talking about?" I asked. "You wear a gun to work and lay your life on the line for us every day!"

Bobby told me this just after speaking to my eighth grade classes. Bobby is a good friend of mine who has served as an officer over the last several years with a police department just outside of Fort Worth, Texas. Bobby risks his life on a daily basis. He is overworked and underpaid, yet he said he could never be a teacher.

Teaching in the public school system in America is becoming more challenging with each passing year. When one considers our ever-changing culture, the depravity our young people are exposed to through various media sources, and the slow disintegration of the family unit, it would be easy for us to throw up our hands and quit. But if we care about young people and the future of our country at all, we know this is not an option.

It was once said, "Hope springs eternal." Rather than waning, my hope for young people today and the future of our country grows by the day. This hope flourishes not just because I am a dreamer but because of the incredible resilience I witness in the lives of my students on a daily basis. Life has handed these young people lemons, and they have made lemonade. They have refused to allow the challenges of life to be an excuse. Many have rejected the peer pressure of friends who would influence them to give up on having a life that matters. They understand they cannot always control what happens in life, but they can control how they respond.

The challenges faced by our young people are greater than ever before. Keeping this in mind, there is one lesson every student in America would do well to master. This lesson is reframing. My first grandson had a bib when he was a baby. On the front of the bib, it read, "Spit Happens." Well, spit happens in life. Reframing is simply viewing negative experiences in our lives differently so we can move forward. Far too many people allow these negative events to define them and affect the rest of their lives. While reframing is one of the most-needed lessons, it is also one of the most challenging for students (and adults) to master. Our kids today are bombarded with such negativity in schools, the media, and at home. If they can learn at such a young age to be optimistic and to find the good in any situation, their lives will be forever changed for the better.

Many of my students have had horrible experiences in their short lives. I try to engrave on their hearts that it is not what happens to a person but how one responds to what happens that makes all the difference. Author and minister, Chuck Swindoll wrote,

> "The longer I live the more I realize the impact of attitude on life. Attitude, to me, is more important than facts. It will make or break a church … a company … a home. The remarkable thing is we have a choice every day regarding the attitude that we will embrace for that day. We cannot change the fact that people will act in a certain way. We can only play on the one string that we have … and that is our attitude. I am convinced that life is 10% what happens to me, and 90% how I react to it."

Several years ago, I was speaking with an acquaintance named Dave. Dave was a psychotherapist from Zimbabwe. We called him "Dave" because we could not pronounce his real name. We were discussing how people from different cultures deal with crises in their lives.

"You Americans are so weak." He could tell from my face I was a little offended, so he continued.

"What I mean is this: it seems like Americans, for the most part, are so easily shaken. They face unexpected crises in their life, and they just shut down emotionally."

I could not argue with his point. He was right. We, in America, are fortunate to live in what I consider the greatest country in the history of the world. Yet because we are so prosperous, we have lost the ability, to a large extent, to deal with crises in a healthy manner.

"Well, Dave, how do you deal with crises in Zimbabwe?"

With a slight grin, Dave said, "In Zimbabwe, we view crises in one way and one way only. We simply view a crisis in our lives as a catalyst for change—nothing more, nothing less."

I was taken aback by the wisdom of those words. Dave's words rang in my ears years later as I held my dad's hand while on his deathbed.

While giving a speech in our class, a girl spoke of how her life was ruined because her dad had left her and her family when she was a baby. Over the next several weeks, we were able to help her understand that her life did not have to be ruined. Her father leaving the family would only ruin her life if she allowed it to ruin her life. Over time, she began to view this event in her life from a different perspective. She now wants to be a child psychologist to help kids who do not have fathers. She has now decided to take this tragedy in her own life and turn it into a positive force for hundreds, perhaps thousands, of other children who may be experiencing abandonment and helplessness.

My most unforgettable "reframing" lesson happened in the fall of 2008. As we were discussing how to reframe the negative experiences in our lives, I gave the students the following prompt: "Write about a time in your life when someone insulted you or was critical of you." I gave them a few minutes to complete the assignment then asked if anyone would be willing to share with the class what he or she wrote. I never force students to share because some of the things they write down are just too painful to talk about in front of the class; however, I have always been surprised at how students are not only willing but eager to share what is happening in their lives.

Michelle raised her hand. She then told us about a summer trip she had taken the previous year to visit her dad. She explained that her dad came home drunk one night and was angry. He said to her that she was an accident and a mistake. He continued saying that he and her mom did not want her, and he wished she had never been born. Tears began to stream down her cheeks like melted wax from a candle. Her set jaw and determination in her eyes made the moment even more emotional. Even though Michelle had presented a strong image to everyone at school, her face at that moment betrayed that image and showed the class there was a wounded little girl behind that strong, have-it-all-together mask.

I paused before responding, partly out of respect for the gravity of what she had just divulged to the class and partly because I was not sure how to respond. As I was gathering my thoughts, David responded from across the room, "How do you reframe that, Coach?" The sarcasm dripping down his chin as he spoke.

I had no answer. So like any master teacher, I challenged the class. "You tell me. How would you reframe it?" My body language and facial expression demonstrated to the class that I had the answer. I just wanted them to discover it for themselves. (We teachers have images we like to uphold as well.) Then Michael raised his hand. "At least your dad was drunk when he told you that. My dad was sober when he said that to me." Then Alisha, who was seated next to Michelle, chimed in. "I went to visit my dad last summer. He told me I was a mistake too. Then he told me he never, ever wanted me and he wished I was dead." At that moment, I felt the lump in my throat swelling. My hands began to shake, and yes, I felt those pesky tears welling up in my eyes. Again, I could not tell if I was more angry or sad. My heart broke for these kids. No child should *ever* hear those words from their father. Although the room was completely silent, the eyes of these kids I had grown so close to were crying out to me for help. I had to respond.

Now at this time, allow me to share some of my personal background, as it is relevant to my response to the students. Much of this background I had already shared with these students. I grew up in a wonderful family. I have never met better parents than mine. I know many people say that about their parents, but I have had several friends over the years claim my parents for their own. My mother stayed home while I was growing up and was the ultimate nurturer. My dad always has been and always will be my hero (more about him in a later chapter). I had an older sister, and although I drove up the wall most days, we always knew deep down we loved each other. Today we are extremely close. I grew up in a Christian home and we went to church every time the doors were open. They were very down-to-earth and simply taught me (mostly by example) how to love God and love people. I felt led to enter "full-time church ministry" while in college and served so faithfully through much of my adult life before entering the world of education several years ago.

Now back to the response; again, with trembling hands and a cracking voice, I told the class to look at me.

"I want everyone's eyes on me. Put down your pencils and close your manuals. And if anyone repeats what I am about to say outside the walls of this room, I will deny it."

This had the effect I was hoping it would have. Every eye was on me, and every student was perfectly still.

I continued, with the most authoritative voice I could muster. "There are no accidents or mistakes in this room! Your parents may not have planned you, but you are not an accident or a mistake. Your parents may not have planned you, but God planned you, and He has a purpose for every single one of you!"

I was surprised by the emotional response from the students. As I looked around the room, close to two-thirds of the class had tears in their eyes. I realized these kids had grown up in the Bible belt and they had never heard anyone tell them that before. I had told church congregations that on Sunday morning more times than I can count, only to see people yawning and dozing off because they had heard it so many times they were immune to it.

I fully understand the guidelines separating church and state, and I respect the laws and rules that set certain boundaries. Yet in that moment, I was compelled to say what I said. I resolved, before I spoke, "If this gets me fired, so be it." In case the reader is wondering, no, I do not beat kids over the head with a sixteen-pound Bible, nor do I try to proselyte or "convert" any of my students. I simply wanted those students to know that they were special. They were living on this earth for a reason. They were not born because of chance, fate, or some cosmic mystery.

That day, a bond was formed between those students and me. I will never forget them. Days like that make teaching worth it. Some of the best lessons learned in school have nothing to do with math, reading, or science, and they cannot be assessed by a state-mandated standardized test. (Did I say that?)

Three weeks after that lesson, Michelle came in the room crying. Her mother had just told her that they were moving across town and she would no longer be attending our school. Saying good-bye to the students is the one part of teaching I hate. She told me we did not have to say our good-byes right then because she was coming back the next day to actually withdraw and would come by my room before she left.

The next day she interrupted my class.

"Good-bye, Coach." Before she could get out any more words, she began to cry. "You're not going to forget me, are you?"

"Not a chance," I replied.

"I will never forget you as long as I live," she muttered through her tears.

I am not sure about her, but I have definitely held up my end of the bargain.

The speed in which technology is advancing today, a year-old laptop is considered a dinosaur. Between Gameboys, smart phones, iPads, iPods, Xboxes and PS3s many students have no time alone, or should I say quiet? This stimulus overload for many has become the norm. As educators, it would behoove us not to dismiss this fact. We are called upon now to do more, and be more, than teachers of '70s and '80s. Not only must we be teachers, now in many cases, we are asked to be mentors, parents, and entertainers. The effective teacher today will find creative ways to both communicate and *connect* with his or her students.

One mode of connection is music. I love music. I play music in my class on a daily basis, especially as the kids enter the room. Much of the music my students listen to would not be considered "school appropriate," so I don't play a lot of their music. I like to go old school on them—after all, I do have white hair. I will play a lot of music from the '50s, '60s, and '70s. One thing I love to do in my class is "Good Things."

During "Good Things" I tell the students to tell me something good that is going on in their lives, with "Tell Me Something Good" playing in the background. We only do it for about three minutes, but it reminds the students that it is important to look for the positive in life. One student shared her story with the class during a speech.

"One day we were doing Good Things. It was about six weeks into the semester. I had never said anything during Good Things, but I was excited about my new CD, so I thought, *What the heck, I'll tell them.* After I told them, everyone clapped for me.

She paused. Her chin slightly quivered. "That was the first time anyone ever clapped for me." She finished the speech wiping tears from her eyes. This little "activity" gave this little thirteen-year-old girl a memory she will never forget.

The content we teach students is vitally important. In order, however, to produce high-performing teams in our classrooms across the country, the students must be convinced their teachers care about more than their grades. Students need to know their teachers care about them as people. In opinion of this writer, a majority of students with failing grades in our country are failing not because they lack the intelligence to succeed but because they lack the motivation to learn. The most important factor in a student's motivation to learn and be successful in school is the relationship he has with his teachers.

In my speech class, we often talk about the power of our words. One lesson deals with the importance of appropriate language. I go on a tirade about some ill of our society. In the middle of my venting, I use the "S" word. A minute later, I ask the kids to comment on what I just said. They don't know if I am asking them to comment on the subject matter or the "S" word. Usually a few students start laughing and tell me I cursed.

"How many of you have heard worse than that in the halls since you have been at school today?" Of course, every hand in the room goes up. "So what's the big deal?" I ask, shrugging my shoulders.

One student exclaims, "You are not supposed to cuss!" Many in the class nod in approval, with the faint sound of yeahs in the background.

"Why am I not supposed to cuss?"

"Because you are a teacher!" several shout simultaneously.

Most of the time, some student will say at this point, "It wouldn't be a big deal if some of the other teachers would cuss, but not you."

"Why?"

"Because you are Coach Bridges; you don't do stuff like that."

"So are you saying that I am like a role model to you guys?" I ask as I am leading them into my snare.

Many in the room respond in the affirmative, either through words or the nodding of their head. At this point, the tables are turned.

"If it is not okay for me to cuss, being an adult, why is it okay for you to cuss?" I ask, speaking progressively slower as I finish the question.

This question is usually met with one of two responses. One response is simple. "It's not okay for us to cuss either."

To be honest, I wish there were many more students who held this view. But many students' language and behavior is a result of what they are exposed to at home on a regular basis. Some of my students tell me they hear their parents drop more curse words in one day than they can count. One day, I confiscated a note two girls were writing each other. As I read the letter, I noticed one girl used the "F" word three times. This was extremely disappointing, because both girls writing the note were wonderful students and I actually could not imagine either one of them using language like that. A few minutes later, the bell rang and I dismissed the class to go to lunch. I walked down the hall toward the cafeteria with Tiffany.

"Hey, Tiffany, what was up with the language you used in the letter? You know better than to talk like that. You are better than that."

A mixture of embarrassment and shame covered her face. She lowered her head and replied is a soft voice, "If that is the only kind of language you hear from your parents every day, sometimes it just comes out. Sorry, Coach."

"You're forgiven," I said. My voice reassured her that I understood. "I am just sorry you have to hear that type of language at home on a regular basis." Unfortunately, her situation is all too familiar to many of my students. A couple of weeks later, she came to me and told me she stopped cursing. It is amazing how a child listens when they are convinced you love them and have their best interests at heart.

Now the second response usually ignites a lively conversation. It goes something like this: "We're just students. It doesn't matter if we cuss. But teachers aren't allowed to cuss."

I always make sure I take time to listen to them and to their (not always logical) reasoning. I once heard a workshop presenter say, "There's not one problem your middle school students will face, that a little reasoning won't make worse." So I listen attentively, answer their questions, and ask some leading questions of my own. I hope to lead them to the conclusions that it is not appropriate anyone to use foul language. I also want them to realize that using positive, appropriate language will not result in negative consequences or cause others to have a negative opinion of you, but using foul language can lead to both. The main point of the lesson is that a person's public life and private life should be consistent. In my class, I teach the students many positive character traits, behaviors, and yes, how to use appropriate language, but the teachings alone would have little effect on my students if I did not practice what I preach. This does not mean that all teachers or parents are going to be perfect. There is an element of hypocrisy in all of us. But it is so important to be consistent. After the discussion, I conclude by asking one more important question. "Be honest with me. How many of you, maybe only for a second or two, were disappointed in me when you heard me say the 'S' word?"

I have yet to see less than 90 percent of the hands raised.

When appropriate adults truly care about kids, and the kids are inspired to fulfill their potential, anything is possible. The key is in the connection. If that connection is made between an appropriate adult and a kid, their future is brighter and hope endures.

We conclude this chapter with a couple of stories written by two of my actual students about their overall experience in our Teen Leadership. You will see the positive changes and renewed hope, all of which was birthed out of a healthy relationship between teacher and student.

Pimples, puberty, and public humiliation in the school cafeteria are just a few of the major things preteens have to worry about in middle school. Now tie that with a pretty bow of depression and you have my life in middle school. I was that kid that wore all black every day. I was absolutely miserable.

When I figured out that I was put in a speech class, I wasn't exactly thrilled.

I did not know exactly what to expect from this class. All I knew was that I was *not* happy about giving speeches in from of the class! I wasn't exactly one who loved to speak in front of people, or even be seen by people, for that matter. I slowly made my way to the new class, carrying the weight of the world on my shoulders. I met Mr. Bridges, a vibrant, happy, and giving man. Throughout the year, we wrote speeches and I had a relatively small class, so we bonded. I remember he would play one song during "Good Things," called "Tell Me Something Good" by Chaka Khan. I looked forward to it!

This class helped me see a different part of life and that it's okay to wear other colors besides black. Now I am a junior (soon to be senior) in high school. I am very involved in my school's theater department, and I'm in varsity choir. I'm in all advanced classes. I'm living my life! I'm being what I want to be. I've got a lot of friends now. I can't walk down the hallway without being stopped by someone! I love to laugh and make people laugh. I've discovered that I love to perform. I doubt I could have figured this out without the help of Mr. Bridges and Teen Leadership.

Sometimes I wonder what life would be like if I didn't take this class. I'd probably still be completely miserable.

Susan

It has been such a joy to watch the literal transformation of Susan over the years. I do not get to see her as much as I would like with her being in high school now, but even if we only see each other across the bleachers at a Friday night football game, we know we shared something special in Teen Leadership, and the choices she is making and will make in the future will continue to pay great dividends.

Everyone has voice in their head. This voice answers your everyday questions like "Paper or plastic?" "Sugar-free or fat-free?" and the eternal "Do these jeans make my butt look fat?" Some people are lucky. They have a smart, self-confident voice. But some people's voice tells them they are stupid, alone, worthless, ugly, and unloved. My voice was like the latter. I think I inherited this trait from my mom, who dealt with abusive men for years because she thought that was all she deserved. It wouldn't be so bad if she had been the only one affected by these choices, but it hurt everyone around her including me. During the day, I smiled and pretended to be okay, but at night, I cried myself to sleep. I soon found myself spiraling into depression. In school I was called "Emo." I slit my wrists, burned my legs, and overdosed on pills. Now before I say anything else, I want to add I didn't get high for the fun of it or for a rush. I wanted my life to end.

But on August 24, 2009, my life took a turn for the better. I started the eighth grade, which meant I started Teen Leadership. Mr. Bridges was like an alarming wake-up call or a painful kick in the butt, which is exactly what I needed. I quit drugs cold turkey and stopped the self-mutilation junk. My smile became real. Now the voice in my head tells me I'm amazing and I'm loved. Oddly enough, this new voice sounds like an old, wise man that knows me better than I know myself.

Misty

In one school year, I saw Misty grow from an insecure, drug-addicted little girl full of anger, bitterness, and depression to a young lady with her entire *positive* life ahead of her. Her gaze is on the future, not her past. She is on the "A" honor roll and made 100 on eight of the nine speeches we did during the semester of Teen Leadership. She earned more 100s than all the other students in all five of my classes combined. She is one of many unsung heroines in my Teen Leadership classes and she now wants to go to college and become a counselor so she can help young people who are facing similar struggles she faced as a child. She has learned the secret of reframing those negative events in her life to make a positive change in her own life, as well as the lives of others.

At the end of her story, she wrote me a personal note that she gave me permission to share.

> Dear Mr. Bridges,
>
> You have changed my life in so many ways. I cannot even begin to describe. Maybe this (story) will help you understand what my life was like before this year. I don't know what I'll do without you, in high school, or in the real world. I will never forget this class or the friends I have made in it. I will ALWAYS stop and think, *Would this be something I would share in "Good Things," and if not, then why am I doing it?* I hope that means a lot to you, because it means a lot to me. My life is so much better now that I know it's worth living. Thank you so much for everything.
>
> Misty
>
> PS: I used an extra large font so you'd be able to read it without difficulty (Ha ha ha)

Did I mention Misty also has aspirations of being a comedian?

As I pen these words, I am reminded of one thing I love about teaching. When I lay my head down on my pillow at night, I never have to wonder if my life made a difference today. As kind as Susan and Misty were in telling their stories, they don't realize that they, along with hundreds of other kids, have given me so much more than I could ever dream of giving them. I love tasting the lemonade made by these young dreamers.

Chapter 2

IT'S A FAMILY AFFAIR

At the end of each semester, the final assignment I give the students is to write me a letter. I ask them to tell me what they liked most about the class, how they thought we could improve the class, how the class has made an impact on their lives, and any other personal note they may like to add. I do not put an emphasis on the length or content of the letter. My primary concern is that they speak from their heart.

As I read the letters, one theme seems to rise above the rest. Approximately 80 percent of the students say what they love about the class is that they can come to our class and just be themselves. It is one of the few places in the world where they do not have to wear masks or try to pretend to be something they are not. Building this kind of family atmosphere that allows the students to be themselves does not happen by accident, nor does it happen overnight. Building a family atmosphere takes patience, vulnerability, and a safe environment.

If a child is fearful about what others will think of them, they are less likely to speak up to answer questions and will (almost) never ask a question in class. The last thing a student wants is to have other students think they are dumb or stupid. They do not realize that if they have a question, there are probably ten other students who have the same question. The others are just too afraid to voice the question in front of their peers. Students will much more likely reach their academic potential if they believe they are free to take risks and ask questions without fear of others judging them or talking about them behind their back.

The establishment of a safe, family atmosphere in the classroom begins before the bell even rings. Between classes, I stand at the door with a big grin on my face, shaking hands with my students as they enter the room. I welcome them and let them know I am glad they came. Sometimes, when I want to have fun, I actually will thank a student for coming to class. They usually look at me like I have lost my mind.

"Why are you thanking me? It's not like I want to be here. I *have* to come."

"Now wait just a minute. That's not true. You chose to be here. The only things you *have* to do are die and pay taxes. You don't *have* to be here."

The student will usually reply with great logic by telling me that if they skipped the class they would get in trouble and possibly face suspension. I assure them that they are correct in their assessment, but they still *chose* to come to class instead of facing the consequences they would face if they skipped the class. I typically end with saying, "You sound like a pretty wise man, if you ask me. I am just really glad you made it today." If nothing else, the student enters the room knowing the teacher is genuinely glad they came to class today. This, in itself, greatly reduces their social anxiety, but it does not necessarily eliminate their anxiety. Many youth today have had the rug pulled out from under them one too many times to trust an adult after one encounter. Many students will watch a teacher over time to see if the teacher is real or just an actor or poser.

Show 'N' Tell

One of the tools we use to help foster a team, or family atmosphere is an old standby called show 'n' tell. We do this simply to give the kids an opportunity to get to know each other. I have the students sit in the floor in a circle. I bring something to share with the class and I actually go first to model what I am looking for in the exercise. I tell the students the following story, as I hold up my dad's binoculars, still in their leather case:

> These are my dad's binoculars. I know they just seem like any other pair of binoculars, but they are very special to me. My dad and I loved TCU football. He was a member of the Frog Club for twenty-five years. We went to several football games each season. We would usually sit in the upper deck and so we needed the binoculars see the action up close. My dad and I loved football, so these were always very special times for both of us.
>
> We also went to the Golden Gloves Boxing Tournaments every year. The regional tournament was held in February and the state tournament was held in March. We would sit in the balcony section of the old Will Roger Coliseum and again would use the binoculars. I remember as a little kid I would pretend I was a TV cameraman and the binoculars were my camera.
>
> We always had a great time, even though I had to walk outside about every twenty minutes to get some fresh air. Back then, there was no smoking ban in public places. Some nights it was hard to even see the ring through all the smoke. Through it all, I always equated the binoculars to very fond memories of my dad. My dad has always been my best friend and my hero.
>
> Several years ago, my dad was diagnosed with prostate cancer. Now when prostate cancer is discovered while still isolated to the prostate, the survival rate is almost 100 percent. Unfortunately, they discovered my dad's cancer too late.
>
> Toward the end of his life, he was home under hospice care. On February 12, 2004, I received a phone call. My

mother told me the doctor instructed her to contact my sister and me and have us come to the house because he only had a couple of days left to live. I packed a duffle bag and drove to their house. Obviously, the doctor failed to take into account that my dad had always been very healthy until this cancer, plus he was a fighter. He lived for sixteen more days. The RN said my dad was an old man, but he was dying like a young man.

About halfway through those sixteen days, my mother wanted me to help her find my dad's living trust papers. My mom is a wonderful woman, but she has never been accused of being an organized, immaculate housekeeper. So finding these papers was no small feat.

While going through one of the bedroom closets, I moved some boxes on one of the shelves. Behind the boxes, I found these binoculars. I said, "Oh my gosh, Dad's binoculars!" I had not seen them for at least twenty years. Without even thinking, I instinctively opened the rawhide leather case and smelled the inside of the case. That leather smell was as fresh as ever. I would never forget the smell because some nights at the fights, I would stick my nose inside the case hoping the leather smell would save me from the smoke that was making me nauseous.

Up until that moment, I had been strong for my mom and my older sister. After all, I was about to be the man of the house—the only man of the house. I would send them out of the room any time Dad needed to go to the bathroom, if he needed pain medicine, or if he was vomiting uncontrollably. I did not want them to have to deal with that, and I knew Dad did not want to put the girls through it either. But the second I smelled that case, a thousand great memories of my dad flooded my mind. I slid down the wall of the closet and sobbed for almost an hour. After that, I left the closet and continued to be

strong for my mom and sister, but I will never forget the
time I spent in that closet as long as I live. And now, these
binoculars sit on the shelf in my closet.

Sometimes when I told the story, I broke down. Sometimes, my
voice would crack, but I successfully kept my composure. Other
times, I showed virtually no emotion at all. It is tough telling that
story six times in a row in one day. Yet it modeled for my students
how to be vulnerable and how to tell a story. And boy, did they have
some stories.

Over the years, I had students bring photos of pets that had died.
A girl would tell the story of how her dog died, while she tried to
hold back the tears. But before she was done, every student who
had lost a pet began to cry with her. Other students would bring
stuffed animals, teddy bears, or other gifts they had received from a
grandfather just before he passed away, which would touch all those
who had lost a grandparent.

By far, the most emotional show 'n' tell was in the fall of 2007.
I had twenty-one students in this particular class. The first seven
students shared their items with little or no emotion. The next
girl had a stuffed animal that was given to her by her grandfather
who had just passed away a month earlier. There were two other
students who lost their grandfathers the previous summer as well.
The floodgates began for four or five of the students.

As we moved around the room, we came to three Latina students
who were best friends. The first girl held up a cloth napkin. On the
napkin was a hand-painted picture of Mother Mary holding Baby
Jesus. As she began to cry, she told us her dad painted this picture and
gave it to her while he was in prison. She went on to tell us he was
still in prison and that she had no idea when he would be released.
The girl next to her held up a similar napkin and picture. She told
us her dad painted it for her also while he was in prison. She began
to weep. "I so wanted my daddy to dance the father/daughter dance
with me at my quinceanera, but he's not eligible for parole for eight

more years." She began to sob. The third friend just had her head down and was already crying. She was unable to speak. There were two more students left. They went quickly out of respect for these three girls who were in so much emotional pain. As I looked around the room, I realized that seventeen of the twenty-one students were crying, including several boys. I asked for eyes of the class to be on me. I was trying to keep my own emotions in check, but my voice was cracking like a twelve-year-old going through puberty.

"I want to tell you guys something you may not hear every day from a teacher. I love you guys. I am sorry you guys have had to face so much tragedy at such a young age. But I want you to know that I care far more about you as people than I care about what grade you receive in my class."

We still had ten minutes left in the class. I told the class they could have free time the last ten minutes, but that I wanted them to be sensitive to the situation since so many students had shared such deeply personal items. For the next eight minutes, the classroom was silent, save for the gasps heard around the room as students did everything they could to stop crying.

For the next eight minutes, I watched that class become a family. Kids were walking across the room hugging other students they barely knew because they shared a common experience. So many of these kids thought they were the only ones going through difficulties; that day, they discovered otherwise. I hardly moved a muscle the whole time. I did not want to risk stopping what I was witnessing before my very eyes.

After the eight minutes, I told the class, "We only have a couple of minutes, so if you guys, especially the ladies, want to freshen up your makeup and pull yourselves together before the bell, you may do so." They thanked me and pulled themselves together as best they could. From that day forward, we were family. We had shared something together that no one could ever take away from us.

Years later, another class had a similar experience with its show 'n' tell. Only this time, it was the boys who were crying uncontrollably.

Four boys were so distraught they could not leave the class. Their issues stemmed back to their fathers. Two of the boys brought gifts their fathers had given them just before their fathers abandoned the family for other women. One of them had not seen his father since the day he received the gift. One other boy brought a birthday present he received from his grandfather shortly before his grandfather's death. The boy's mom and dad were both in prison, so his grandfather raised him up until his death.

I coach football at our school as well, and I had to miss the first forty-five minutes of practice because the boys in my seventh-period class refused to leave. They had reputations to uphold and there was no way they could salvage their reputation in their current condition. I watched, in amazement, as these boys took strides in becoming men. They comforted each other and encouraged each other. They understood that the tears they shed that day were in no way a sign of weakness. On the contrary, the tears were symbolic of the strength they exhibited every day. Even though these hurts were always with them, they lived their lives and refused to let their past dictate their future. I have never been one for superficial demonstrations of emotion, but I told these young men that after knowing what they had been through, crying was the only appropriate response.

Once they gathered themselves, I wrote them passes to their next classes. That semester, my seventh-period class was my highest performing class. Much of that was due to the fact that they were, and still are, family.

Building Family in the Classroom

So far, you have read a few stories of my students and will read about many more throughout this book. When people hear these stories, they often ask me specifically what transpired in the class to cause the remarkable changes in the lives of these kids. It is difficult to pinpoint one particular day or lesson that made the dramatic change. I believe it is a combination of several factors, not the least of which is "building family." This is a challenge when working in a school in which many students have a negative view of family. Sometimes, I have to talk to the students about us building a "healthy" family. We then discuss what a healthy family looks like. How does a healthy family talk to one another? How does a healthy family treat one another? Can a healthy family trust one another? Can they keep a secret? Is a healthy family loyal to each other? It is very important to describe that for which we are striving. Interestingly, during this discussion, students often refer to our social contract. To illustrate this point, over the last twelve months of the writing of this book, I have had eleven students tell me they were on drugs when they started attending my class. Several of them said they quit doing drugs a couple of weeks into the semester because of Teen Leadership. The only things we discuss the first two weeks of the semester are classroom procedures and the social contract. Many of them quit using drugs because for the first time in their lives they felt like they have a group of people that truly loved and cared about them.

A couple of years ago, during show 'n' tell, Joey began to cry as he told us about his grandfather. He was holding up some medals his grandfather earned in the Vietnam War. His grandfather gave him the medals just before he died. As he finished telling us the story of his grandfather, he began to cry uncontrollably. This was the first time Joey ever spoke up in front of the class. Joey was Caucasian and was one of our special-education students. He was one of the largest students in our school. Most of the students in the class had seen Joey teased, laughed at, or bullied in the halls many times (some of them probably participated in the teasing). So when Joey broke down, the awkwardness (and guilt) seemed to paralyze the entire class. Well, it paralyzed the entire class except JC. JC was an African American student who was the class clown who had perfected his craft. One thing that added to his humor was his size. JC was about five feet two and dreamed of the day he would reach one hundred pounds.

As Joey was sitting on the floor, crying with his face buried in his hands, trying desperately to hide himself from the other students, JC slowly walked from across the room. He knelt down in front of Joey. JC then positioned Joey's head where it was resting on his shoulder. He softly repeated, "It's going to be okay, Joey. It's going to be okay." JC comforted Joey with these words while slowly rubbing the top of Joey's head. It was one of the most beautiful scenes I had witnessed in all my years of teaching (or pastoring a church, for that matter).

As beautiful as this scene was, middle school students have a limited capacity for public demonstrations of emotions and affection. Some of the students became uneasy and were looking to me to intervene. "Mr. Bridges, do something!" I was doing something. I was thoroughly enjoying the moment while attempting to swallow the "baseball-sized" lump in my throat. I was preparing to say something to appease the uncomfortable students in the room when JC turned and looked at me. A tear was falling from the corner of his eye like a drop of dew falling from a blade of grass. "Mr. Bridges, someone has to comfort him, don't they?" I simply nodded and smiled.

The class learned a lesson that day they would not have learned in a week's worth of lectures. I know it might seem like academics are not a priority to me as a teacher. Nothing could be farther from the truth. Many teachers feel they do not have enough time to become emotionally involved with their students. They have too much content to teach, not to mention the additional requirements of the state, which seem to increase with each passing year. Teachers are often asked what they teach. Most teachers reply with their grade level or their content area. When people ask me what I teach, I simply tell them I teach students. Teachers are only teaching when the students are learning. Do you think students will learn more if they are in a class where they like the other students in the class and have a great relationship with the teacher, or will they learn more in an environment based on intimidation and fear? This fear can be a fear of the teacher or a fear of the other students making fun of them.

I once had a teacher (I will call her Ms. Johnson) approach me during lunch. She asked me if I could sit in on her class during my conference period and give her some feedback.

"I would be glad to," I replied. "But why do you want me to observe you?"

"Well, my classes aren't going very well, and every time I call my kids 'morons' or tell them to shut up, someone always raises their hand and says, 'Mr. Bridges never talks to us like that.'" The last part was said with a definite whiney and nasally tone. I, of course, agreed, keeping my ear-to-ear grin on the inside.

The next day, I sat in on Ms. Johnson's class. I found a seat where I used to sit in my classes in high school—the far back corner of the room. I did not want to draw attention to myself so the class would carry on as usual. Ms. Johnson checked attendance at her computer while the class was doing bell work. There were a few whispered conversations, but nothing disruptive. Ms. Johnson came to the overhead, slammed down her math book and said, "Shut up, pay attention, and let's get started," with a scowl on her face.

She covered the lesson very thoroughly. Ms. Johnson was brilliant, yet her students' scores consistently ranked among the lowest in the school. As she continued explaining the new concepts of the lesson, a student had a question. After the student asked the question, Ms. Johnson rolled her eyes and told the student she already covered that and he should pay attention. The student received no help. A few minutes later, a student asked a question that many in the class viewed as a "dumb question." Another student made a brash comment tearing down the student that asked the question. For the first time, I saw Ms. Johnson laugh. Too bad it was at the expense of one of her students. As the class was coming to an end, *I* was afraid to be in the class. There was absolutely no safety—emotionally, socially, or otherwise. When the bell rang, students almost sprinted to the door. They wanted to leave as quickly as possible.

Once the students cleared the room, Ms. Johnson slowly walked back toward my seat while shaking her head. She flopped down in the desk next to mine.

"Well, how bad was it?" she asked, expecting the worst.

"Do you *like* kids?" I asked curiously.

"What do you mean?"

"I mean, *do you like kids?*" I repeated very emphatically. "The only time I saw you laugh, or even smile, the entire class, was when one kid put another kid down in front of the whole class, and you laughed with everyone else."

She sheepishly looked down toward the floor as if she were a little girl whose father just caught her in a lie. I continued. "It doesn't seem like you show any respect to the kids at all. I see the social contract on the wall, but I don't see you following it."

"Well, if those kids aren't going to respect me, I ain't gonna respect them!"

I was touched by such a loving sentiment from a colleague. "That's the difference between you and me. I am going to respect them whether they respect me or not, because my respecting them is about me. It does not depend on how well, or how poorly, my students treat me." I was hoping this would clarify for her the importance of love and respect in the classroom.

She then became somewhat defensive. "Well, I guess I'm not the perfect, loving teacher you are. I am not that much of a people-person."

"Ms. Johnson, it is not about being perfect or being a people-person. It is about choices. I choose to love and respect my students before I even meet them on the first day of school. *We* are the adults in the relationship. Many of these kids will never understand what it means to love and respect others if we do not demonstrate those things to them as their teachers. You and I both know many of these kids will never see it at home."

We talked for over an hour, and it was very fruitful conversation. I offered some very practical action steps she could take to start building a healthy relationship with her students. I would check on her from time to time, and I did not always hear favorable comments from her or her students, although we had developed a very cordial relationship with each other. Our personalities were nothing alike, yet we maintained a mutual respect for one another, both as colleagues and friends.

Toward the end of the school year, we received word that several teachers would be forced to change rooms the next school year, so we would have to move our personal belongings before we left for summer break. I walked by Ms. Johnson's room the last day of school after the students had left. She was packing boxes.

"Which room are they moving you to?" I asked, offering to help move things for her.

She paused, staring into a box she was packing. "I was told today that my services are no longer needed here."

I shared with her my regret and asked her if there was anything I could do for her. She was very gracious and thanked me for all I had already done for her, and we parted ways. Ms. Johnson was relieved of her duties not because of her lack of knowledge, or even because of her personality. She was primarily lost her job because she refused to choose to love and respect her students. As Flip Flippen says, "If you have a child's heart, you have his head."

In the classroom, it is sometimes difficult to build family when so many students come from unhealthy, dysfunctional homes. The more dysfunctional the home, the more difficult it is for the students to love others and receive love. Some of the most disrespectful, rude behavior I have encountered from students has been following my going to extraordinary lengths to reach out to them. If a student does not know how to receive love, they will often behave in such a way as to push away the very person who is showing them love. When the person walks away, the student says to himself or herself, "I knew they were just like everyone else." By behaving in this manner, the student can at least control how and when others reject them.

Fortunately, for every sad story of a student rejecting help from me, or anyone else, there are a hundred stories of kids who chose to change their lives for the better. I have seen kids who have undergone unspeakable horrors of abuse make commitments to be the best parents they can be. Some of my students will be the first in their family to graduate from high school, and they are planning to graduate from college as well. They are going to stop the pattern of abuse and poverty that has plagued their families for generations. I tell my students often that many of them have tragic stories, but by choosing to follow the same path as their parents, they are eliminating any opportunity for their lives to inspire anybody. No one wants to hear a story about a kid who makes the same poor choices his parents have made. That's not a story. It is easy to follow the parents' poor choices when one is raised in such horrible conditions. Anyone can be just another statistic. The real stories are students who overcome those things and move forward. The students need to understand that while I care what has happened to them growing up, their future employers are not going to care. They will simply want to see results. So when they give in to self-pity, they are only hurting themselves.

Even though not all my kids have fairy-tale endings, I believe the change-agent in my classes that has impacted so many students' lives is our ability to "build family." As I tell the students, this is not rocket science or brain surgery. Building family is choosing to love, respect, and serve each other. Jesus said, "No greater love has any man than this, than he that lay down his life for his friends." Building family is about laying down your life for another. It is about putting the interests of others ahead of your own.

Building Family at Home

Putting others' interests ahead of your own holds true if one is "building family" in the classroom *or* at home. At home, I have three daughters and one wife. At the time of this writing, my wife and I are about to celebrate thirty glorious years of marriage. Our marriage is not perfect. It takes a tremendous amount of work and constant attention. Yet thirty years after I said, "I do," I still get a few butterflies when I see her from across the room. I will not delve into all the trials we have faced as a couple and as parents (perhaps that will be for another book), but our love for each has grown through it all.

I have three daughters who have been the joy of my life. My wife and I are now empty nesters. My youngest is attending college at Baylor University. Her older sisters have already graduated from Baylor. All three of them were high achievers, graduating in the top 10 percent of their class and excelling in cheerleading as well as music and theater. My oldest daughter is married to a wonderful young man. We do not feel like we have lost a daughter. We have gained a son. And those two have given us our first grandson. Yes, I finally got that boy!

My wife and I have incredible relationships with our daughters. We love spending time with them. We also pride ourselves in being our children's greatest cheerleaders. We have never told them they had to get straight A's in class, but we have demanded their very best effort. Naturally, their best efforts have almost always resulted in A's, even in college. They are overachievers in many ways, not because they have something to prove but because we have trained them to give 100 percent effort toward whatever they choose to do. Also, because we have never made a correlation between their performance and our love and acceptance of them as parents, all three of our daughters have a healthy self-esteem and have no problem taking risks to achieve their goals.

This very brief history of our family serves as a backdrop for how I teach my students. I teach my students much the same way I have raised my children. As a result, it is somewhat easy to build this family atmosphere. Since so many of my students come from broken homes, I speak frequently about my family, hoping to demonstrate the type of family they could have someday.

A few years ago, one of my classes only had one girl in the entire class. Her name was Danielle. She was a fireball, so she held her own quite well with the sixteen male classmates she had to engage regularly. Danielle was quite unique in many ways. Most people at school would consider her a Goth. She had black hair, black shirt, black hoodie, black pants, black shoes, black eyeliner, black lipstick, and black fingernails. She often spoke of vampires and death. Yet on the other hand, she was incredible student (all A's) and was quite enjoyable to talk to once you got past the harsh outward image she portrayed. The friends Danielle surrounded herself with looked like her clones. Yet there was only one major difference. While Danielle excelled in school and had great interpersonal skills, her friends, for the most part, did not care about school or what they were going to do with their lives. Several times during the school year, I would walk by them in the hall only to hear Danielle, grilling her friends, asking them if they completed their homework and if they had studied for their tests. Many people however, would not give Danielle a chance because of her friends and her appearance. On many occasions, I had to remind Danielle that it was not right that people judged her because of her appearance and the company she kept, but it was just a reality.

"That's just how the real world is, Danielle. First impressions are very important and people will, for the most part, judge you on that first impression, which includes how you dress and with whom you choose to be friends. I am not telling you to dress differently or choose other friends; I am just saying as long as you dress like this and hang out with the friends you hang out with, people are going to unfairly judge you. It is simply a reality you are going to have to come to grips with. If you don't, those judgments will lead to you becoming bitter and casting judgments on others."

One day in our class, toward the end of the semester, we were talking about home and family issues and I asked Danielle if I could ask her a personal question. She nodded and said, "Sure, go for it."

"I have told you guys a lot about my family, about my wife, and how we raise our children. Right?"

"Yeah," she replied.

"How do you think your life would be different if you were raised in my home?" I asked the question while fully expecting the typical middle school response: "I 'ono." (Or properly translated, "I don't know.") Her response surprised me.

She stared at me with a poker face that seemed to say, "I have a royal flush. Try me."

She retorted, "I wouldn't dress like this, and I wouldn't hang out with the friends I hang out with."

"Why not?"

"I wouldn't want to." At that moment, the bell rang. She picked up her binder, wiping a tear from her eye as she quickly left the room. That was the first sign of emotion I had seen in her all semester, which is saying something for a teenage girl.

I later took her to speak at a CKH conference. The teachers could not believe their eyes. They even judged her before she spoke. When Danielle's speech was over, many teachers owed her an apology. It was a good lesson for all of us about the danger of judging a book by its cover. Honestly, that was a lesson Danielle taught me firsthand.

I have been fortunate to experience success both as a teacher/coach and a father. I believe being good at one makes me better at the other. Being a good father has helped me truly care about my students. I treat them much the same way I treat my own daughters. I joke with the girls, telling them I must approve all boyfriends. Many of the girls do not have fathers at home so they appreciate someone looking out for them. I try to help the young men understand what it takes to grow up to be a man of integrity. It is next to impossible for a single mother to teach a boy how to be a man. I am unable to do all I would like for my students, but that does not stop me from doing what I can.

As a parent, one may need to adapt how they apply these principles at home, but the principles do not change.

Listen. Earlier I mentioned having my students write me a letter as their last assignment. One of the most common remarks about what they liked is that I took time to listen to their troubles and what is actually going on in their lives.

Take time to listen to your children, especially during their pivotal teen years. If your family is like most, when the children reach middle school and high school life becomes more chaotic, both physically and emotionally. Children are met with challenges they have not had to face before. There is also a tendency for children to feel like they are the only ones going through whatever it is they are experiencing. They are the only one who has ever been dumped by a boyfriend or girlfriend. They are the only teenager in America to have a pimple on the end of their nose that makes them look like Rudolf, the red-nosed reindeer.

Be a role model. I mentioned earlier I spent years in full-time church ministry. My biggest fear about being a preacher was not preaching in front of a crowd. My biggest fear was having "preacher's kids" (PKs). When I was in school, the worst kids were the sons and daughters of preachers. The main reason for this is that the image the preacher presented on Sunday morning was not the father at home on Sunday afternoon. Children today are not going to respect a parent who says one thing and does something else. In fact, recent studies have found that hypocrisy is so widespread that young people almost expect it. Have the courage and character to look your children in the eye and say, "Watch me. Live your life like I live mine." Would you currently want your children following your example? Most likely, they already are.

Spend time with your children. This does not mean that you stay in the same house but that you truly engage your children and give them your undivided attention. One tradition I started in my family was what we referred to as "Daddy Dates." When my daughters were in their early elementary years, I realized that there would come a time when they would become teenagers and they may not think Daddy knows everything like they do when they are younger. So I decided while they were hanging on every word Daddy spoke that I would take advantage of it and teach them how to conduct themselves on a date and what should be expected by the young man taking them on the date.

I would walk my daughter to the car. As she reached for the door handle, I would abruptly say, "Don't touch that handle. You stand by the door and wait for your date to open the door for you." I would then open the door for her and instruct her to say thank-you to the young man before she is seated. As we drove in the car, I would model for my daughter how to engage a young man in a conversation. I would usually talk about whatever they wanted to talk about, but then I would tell them boys like to talk about themselves. I would then give them some questions they could ask a boy to initiate a conversation. One of the most effective was this: "Have you been working out?" Boys fall for that one every time.

As we would park the car at the restaurant, my daughter would instinctively reach again for the door handle. Again, I would tell her to sit there until the young man comes around the car and opens the door for her. My daughters would always ask, "But what if he doesn't open the door for me?"

"Then you sit there until he does," I would reply in a strong voice.

"What if he just walks in the restaurant?"

"Then you take the quarter in your purse and call me and I will come get you." This was before cell phones. So it is easy for my youngest. She has a cell phone.

Of course, I am a believer in preemptive strikes, so I always have a talk with the young men about how my daughter is to be treated. So far, my daughters have never had the need to call me. One day, Trevor, who is now my son-in-law, came to pick up my oldest daughter, Shannon, for a date. They had been dating two years and he had just proposed to her. I still needed to make sure he was treating my daughter like a princess. So I spied on them through the front blinds. Trevor walked Shannon to the car. Shannon stopped.

Trevor opened the door for her and made sure the hem of her dress was inside the car before he closed the door. Trevor learned well.

So whether you are a teacher or a parent, building family is probably the most important job you have. As a father, the two most important things I can give my children are roots and wings. The roots bring stability, safety, and comfort in a troubled world. Wings allow them to soar with the eagles and reach their full potential, without being debilitated by a fear of failure or rejection. Building family supplies them with both.

When a family atmosphere is established in a classroom, student performance increases naturally. We all have had classes in school we enjoyed and classes we would like to forget. Anyone who reflects objectively on these classes will most likely find that the classes they enjoyed were the ones that had a family atmosphere. In most cases, one would find a rise in academic scores in those classes that felt like family. Human nature tells us that we perform better when we feel safe and are encouraged. In fact, the rest of this book was built on the foundation of "building family." To adequately reach today's youth, it may be necessary for teachers revisit the tried-and-true methods of thirty years ago. Establishing a family atmosphere is essential for the success of any classroom. A family atmosphere surpasses motivation to learn. A family atmosphere motivates children to become lifelong learners.

Chapter 3

THE PERFECT STORM
(ALSO KNOWN AS SECOND PERIOD)

Billy Tyne, the captain of the *Andrea Gail,* and his crew were fishing for swordfish in the Grand Banks off the shores of New England. *Andrea Gail* became caught in the largest storm in recorded history. The storm was formed when three major storm systems converged off the New England shores. Billy Tyne, his crew, and the *Andrea Gail* were never heard from again. Most Americans became familiar with Billy Tyne and his crew after watching the movie *The Perfect Storm,* which stars George Clooney.

If there was an educational equivalent to the perfect storm, it was my second-period class a few years ago. August rolled around and I awoke from my summer slumber. As I perused the roster for my second-period class, my heart sank and my blood pressure rose. Some of the students I had coached the previous year, and other students I simply knew by reputation. After the first two days of school, I discovered there were half a dozen students who made me want to pull out what little hair I have left. Almost half of the students were loud, unruly, and disrespectful. By the end of the first week, I knew this class would be the challenge of my teaching career.

The entire first week of school I focused solely on was classroom procedures. If I failed to establish discipline early on, it would be a long semester indeed. As each new procedure was introduced, student commentaries could be heard across the room, usually in the form of a mumble. The most common comments were "This is stupid" and the infamous "Why do we have to do bell work anyway?" The latter was always accompanied with a whiney voice.

One of my personal procedures is to stand at the door each day, shaking hands with my students as they enter the room. When the bell rang to end first period, I would take a deep breath and say a short prayer. The prayer was usually simple and went something like this: "Oh God, help!" Or this: "Lord, don't let me do anything during second period that would get me fired." I then proceeded to open the door and greet each student with the brightest smile I could muster. Almost half the kids would shake my hand. The others would walk by as though I was not even standing there, looking at my hand like it was covered with some sort of fungus. I was determined not to let them get to me, however. Nothing would give them more pleasure than to see me lose my temper. In their eyes, that would simply prove I was a hypocrite. I later learned that a dad, an uncle, or some other male authority figure emotionally or physically abused many of them. As a class, they found it difficult, if not impossible, to trust any man.

There were three young men who took it upon themselves to discover and push every button I had on a daily basis. Defiance, disrespect, and constant disruptions were a daily occurrence. They were good friends and definitely fed off each other. I would like to say it was a totally different class when these three were either absent or suspended, but they were only three of a dozen students who made me earn my money as an educator.

The real fireworks began in our class less than three weeks into the semester. Two of the girls in the class were best friends. Their names were Karen and Anna. They were joined at the hip for the first week or two. Then one day, they came into the class separately, and both looked angry. Well, I may have been born at night, but it was not last night. I concluded that these two young ladies were at odds with one another. I asked them in front of the class what was wrong and they proceeded to tell me in very colorful terms, but I decided to address their language at a later date. This may come as a shock to many readers who have middle school aged daughters, but they were fighting about a boy.

As they were both stating their case, I drew the class's attention to the social contract displayed on the wall. I reminded the students how they said they would treat each other when there was conflict. Most of the answers when we developed the social contract were "listen, talk it out, be mature, Golden Rule," etc. So I asked Anna and Karen if they would mind if we actually practiced these things in front of the class so we could demonstrate how to deal with conflict in a mature, healthy way. Surprisingly, they both agreed.

They began talking rather loudly, and then I reminded them to listen to the other before responding. I started asking them some clarifying questions to make sure we all understood what was being said. Although it was rather tense for a while, and we had several of the students laughing during the process, Anna and Karen worked it out and even asked the other's forgiveness. Neither of these girls had a reputation of being forgiving or understanding. So when the dust settled, several students were looking at each other with a quizzical look as if to say, "What just happened?"

Karen asked, "Hey, Coach, how did you do that?"

"Do what?"

"You know, get us to work everything out."

"You guys worked it out. I just asked questions that helped you stay on topic instead of making it personal." Most of these students had never had seen anyone handle a conflict in a healthy manner. I then began to talk to the students about my own marriage and how my wife and I had dealt with conflict over the years.

"Don't you think my wife and I have had conflicts since we have been married for twenty-something years?" I asked rhetorically. "Healthy marriages are not conflict-free. But people with healthy marriages know how to resolve conflicts while maintaining mutual respect and love. Even at our angriest moments, my wife and I know we will work through whatever it is that is causing the anger. The most important aspect of our relationship is that we both know we are totally committed to the relationship."

While this class was the source of more than a few of my gray hairs, I grew to love each and every one of these students. Our discussions were usually much deeper than the other classes'. This is because of the difficult situations these students were forced to deal with at such a young age. For many of them, their innocence was taken from them at a very early age. I decided a few years ago that becoming angry with my students for their misbehavior was futile. I knew if I lost control of my temper that most of the students would view this as a victory. Over time, I learned about their background and their family life. Several times, I had to force myself to maintain a straight face while they told their stories. I learned a few years ago that there was no reason to be angry with my students for acting out. Their behavior was only a symptom. The root cause of their behavior and attitude was what they had to face at home on a daily basis. This concept held true for my second-period class as well. Actually, the intensity of the stories of this class is what prompted me to devote an entire chapter to them. Here are only a few of their stories.

Bradley

Bradley was a young man who, at first glance, would not make a teacher leap for joy because he was in their class. To this day, I do not know what color his eyes are because it is hard to see them through all the hair. His pants were sagging, his shirttail was out, and he carried an air about him that shouted, "I'm too cool for school!" Although he would talk a little more than he should, he would not cause too many problems in class. He did not disrupt the class, but he did not do anything else either. Bradley was failing the class simply because of the number of zeros he had accumulated. Honestly, reaching out to Bradley was difficult. My wife had had Bradley in her class in sixth grade. He was such a terror in her class that he caused her to leave the room crying three different times. As the semester progressed, however, Bradley slowly began to divulge details about his background.

Bradley's mom became pregnant with him when she was sixteen years old. When Bradley's father found out she was pregnant, he performed an escape routine that would make Houdini proud. Bradley's mother turned to drugs to try to cope with her desperate situation. Bradley once told me, "I was about four or five years old when I found the first bag of weed in my mom's room." At that point, Bradley and his mother were forced to leave his grandmother's house in which they were living at the time. Over the next two years, they lived in approximately ten different homes. They were extremely poor because Bradley's father never paid child support. His dad was arrested and put on probation for ten years. Despite all of this, Bradley maintained straight A's in elementary school.

One day, Bradley mentioned how he used to get straight A's in elementary school. Now by the eighth grade, when he came to Teen Leadership, his average grade was around seventy. He did just enough to pass, but sometimes he even fell short of that lofty goal. I told him I always knew he was smart. I asked him what happened to change his academic performance. Bradley also recounted a story for me that he said changed to course of his life.

"When I was about eleven years old, I saw my mom's former boyfriend punch her in the face, so I hit him in the face. As a result, I was sentenced to five months probation. Since that day, nothing has ever been the same and never will be." Bradley thought he was sentenced for simply defending his mother.

Over the next several weeks, Bradley and I worked on changing the current path he was taking. At the end of the semester, I had all my students write me a letter. I wrote all 127 students back. I wanted them to know that I cared about each one of them individually. When the course was over, Bradley wrote another letter describing his experience in Teen Leadership.

This year in eighth grade Teen Leadership, I have learned so much about life. I have learned about forgiveness and family. Coach Bridges is the best teacher I have ever had, no questions asked. Coach wrote me a letter, and in his letter he said, "I want to encourage you to fight whatever it is inside you that makes you not want to try and not care. I don't want you to be my age and look back with regrets." That showed me he really cared. My mom has now found a great man. We have a nice house and good family. As for my father, he still won't talk to me. Teen Leadership has helped me tremendously. THANK YOU, Coach.

Bradley

For the teachers out there, it is important to note that Bradley never gave any indication whatsoever that he even listened to anything I said all semester. Therefore, reading his letter was one of the highlights of my school year. The teaching profession is much more about planting seeds than harvesting crops. Unfortunately, many teachers are never privileged to see the full impact they may have had on the lives of their students.

Maria

One of the most intense speeches the students give during the semester is titled "A Memorable Experience." One day while Maria was giving her speech, she told us a family relative molested her when she was young. She spoke about the guilt that incident brought on and the isolation it caused her to feel.

When that happened, I asked myself, "Why me?" I thought the entire incident was my fault. I didn't know why, but I felt like I wasn't good enough to be normal, so I would just have to live with this awful secret. Sometimes I feel so alone.

I have a good life. My mom takes good care of me, but my dad isn't there. But still it's there—the hurt of not belonging, thinking that what I have to say is not important. Deep down I know it is, but I just don't speak up.

Several weeks later, Maria wrote me a letter describing her experience in the class.

Sometimes the feeling of isolation is enough to cause me not to talk. But during Teen Leadership, I realized that I needed to tell my story so I wouldn't feel the isolation. Telling my story has helped others in my class that experienced similar types of abuse. I now feel like I am in control of my life instead of this awful secret being in control. Plus I have forgiven the person who abused me. I learned this lesson and many others in Coach Bridges' Teen Leadership class.

But the thing I will never forget (even if I get Alzheimer's) is the strange feeling of "familyness" that could only come from blood. But oddly, in this class, we are not blood, but the family feeling is still there.

Maria mentioned a significant lesson she learned in Teen Leadership that most adults never learn. She stated in her letter that she learned to forgive the man who sexually molested her. An untold number of victims of this type of abuse vehemently declare, if not publicly then at least to themselves, that they will *never* forgive the person who abused them. And who could blame them? If someone sexually abused one of my daughters, I would want to visit them while wielding a rather large baseball bat. I explained to the students, however, that by clinging to bitterness and refusing to forgive, they are only hurting themselves. I wish I could say Maria was the only abuse victim in my class, but that was far from the truth.

Katrina

Katrina joined our class late, transferring from another school across town. Katrina's joining our class was almost like pouring kerosene on a fire. It seemed the boys thought Katrina was cute. Unfortunately, the boys who were most attracted to her were the boys in the class that caused the greatest disruptions. Although Katrina joined in on the festivities, and was quite disruptive at times, she never showed me any disrespect, unlike the other three gentlemen. Things seemed to be growing from bad to worse. Then over the next several months, the other three boys made decisions that led to a change in schools, specifically our alternative school. Meanwhile, Katrina seemed to be making better choices and I noticed I was seeing a genuine smile on her face more often. Her grade was improving and it actually seemed as though she was enjoying school.

During "family time" one day, Katrina alluded to some traumatic experiences she had endured before transferring to our school. I asked her, after class, if she felt comfortable telling me her story. She said she would feel better writing it down. She did not want to forget anything, plus it was still difficult for her to talk about.

Katrina said her mother was on drugs when she became pregnant with Katrina and stayed on drugs throughout the pregnancy. Her father was there, but when he saw that Katrina had blonde hair, he denied that she was his daughter. A couple of months later, he went to prison for seven years. This entire time, her mother continued to get drunk seemingly every night. Katrina went on to state in her letter that her mother continued to get drunk and do drugs on a regular basis. She endured abuse from her mother's boyfriend and witnessed her mother being abused. Finally, it ended when the police were called to intervene because Katrina and her mother literally feared for their life. Here is how Katrina concluded her letter.

> I never will forgive my mom for going back with this guy.
> It has messed up a lot in my life and now I live with my
> dad who may not even be my real dad.

Since then, Katrina has continued to take control of her life and make the choices that will help her become the woman she wants to be. The family atmosphere of our class had a major impact on her ability to move forward. She has heard many of the stories of other students in the class and realized that she is not alone. The loneliness and isolation are primary causes of drug addiction and alcohol abuse among teenagers today. When they have a strong support system including both adults they can trust and friends who are urging them to make wise choices, the number of substance-abuse cases drops dramatically.

After a few weeks, I realized I would have to take some unique steps to reach my second-period class. One day as the students entered the room, they saw several words on the whiteboard. These words represented trials and challenges the kids had been forced to deal with at some point in their lives. The words included *alcoholism, drug addiction, betrayal, unforgiveness, physical abuse, sexual abuse, poverty, divorce, stress, drama* (you know how middle schools are), plus a few others. The assignment was to write a two-page essay on at least two of these challenges and two action steps they could take to overcome each one. There was a great need for them to understand that if they had experienced some difficulties at home, their boss is not going to care. The boss will only care about how well they are doing their job. Many students have no problem discussing these challenges in their lives, but few of them take a proactive approach toward overcoming these challenges. As I was reading these assignments, one in particular stood out among the rest.

Angela

Angela wrote her essay about divorce and alcoholism. Her mom's alcoholism was one of the contributing factors to her parents' divorce.

Angela joined us in January for the spring semester. It was difficult changing school immediately following Christmas, but Angela adjusted well and quickly made friends in the class. I also noticed the friends she chose were some exceptional students who worked hard every day and whose choices were helping them achieve their dreams and goals. I had always been impressed with Angela. After I read Angela's essay, my being impressed was upgraded to admiration.

Alcoholism is a situation I'm dealing with right now. My mom and stepfather are alcoholics. Due to my mom's alcoholism, I am not allowed to be alone with her and my stepfather at their house. Over Christmas break, they got drunk every day.

One day they were fighting. I went out by the dock so I would not have to hear them. A few minutes later, I ran in the house because I heard a loud "boom." When I entered the house, I found my mother on the floor. I called my stepfather's brother who came to get me. He took my mother and me to another brother's house. From there, I called my dad to come get me. When I told him what happened, I could hear him begin to cry. That made the entire ordeal even more emotionally trying.

Just when I thought it could not get any worse, I was sitting in the computer room, waiting for my dad, when I heard a loud noise outside and people yelling. So I went outside to see what was happening, only to hear my stepfather threaten to kill my mom. I screamed at him to leave us alone and go away. Reluctantly, he left.

I had to stay strong for my mother because she told me she had nothing to live for. I talked to her and calmed her down, but I also told her that if she were still with him when I had kids, I would not let my children come see her. I thought that would change her mind about staying with this guy, but it didn't.

When my dad and two other people came to get us, my mom said she wanted to go back home. When we got home, my mom and dad were talking off to the side of the porch. I was sitting on the porch in the porch swing. My stepfather came to the door with a gun. I told my dad and he talked to my stepfather and convinced him to put the gun down. I then went inside and collected my things and my dad and I left.

I worried about my mother the whole ride home. But I realized I could not allow alcoholism or anybody get me down, especially if it is a parent. You have to be there for them, keep them strong, and get them through it.

I have tried to forgive my stepfather, but it's hard. I am forgiving him gradually, because if I don't forgive him it will hurt me more than him. If I allow hate and unforgiveness to grow inside me, it will destroy me. People just need to understand that they need to forgive those who hurt them even if their story is worse than mine because holding grudges only hurts you.

What wisdom from such a young lady. She learned a lot about forgiveness in our class, but she was well on her way to recovery when she came to our class. Her strength of character stands as an example to us all. She had every reason to give up on her own life. After all, why should she care when her mom did not? Most teenagers in her situation would to turn to alcohol or drugs for at least a temporary reprieve from the pain. They do not realize that after the high, the pain returns, usually with greater intensity that results in a deeper level of depression. Yet Angela has chosen to keep her eyes on the prize rather than on the obstacles *to* the prize. This is a girl I want to check on in fifteen years. She will be doing something life changing!

Karen

Earlier I mentioned a girl named Karen. She was one of girls in the conflict about a boy that we resolved in front of the class. When I first met Karen on the first day of school, I knew I had my work cut out for me. Barely five feet tall, was she a little stick of dynamite. She was loud, talkative, and funny, but then she could turn in an instant and freeze people with her stare. I thought about nicknaming her Medusa, but I did not want to hurt her feelings. Our relationship seemed to get off to a good start, but I could tell there were the rumblings of a volcano just below the surface. The first week of school, I could tell she was a leader. I believed if I could reach her, I could reach anyone in the class. If I could reach her, several others would follow. I focused in on Karen. I felt like she had a difficult home life and knew if I were too hard on her I would lose her and probably the whole class.

In my attempts to reach her, I gave her a little more leeway than usual. As a result, several students accused me of playing favorites. I did not see it that way. I was very purposeful in what I was doing. It was strategic. Yet I could easily see how these students would feel like I treated Karen as my favorite. She would often come to my desk during class and talk to me about things at home. When we had family time, Karen would often dominate the conversation. Students in other classes wrote me letters during the semester thanking me for never having favorites in my class. This was the first time I had ever been accused of favoritism. In reflecting over our time together, I had to admit there was merit to the students' accusations. I wrote letters of apology to the students who felt that I was playing favorites.

In the process of writing this book, I wanted to include Karen's story because of the positive changes I have seen take place in such a short time. I knew she could share her story better than I could. So here is Karen's story in her own words.

At first glance, I seem normal: a normal girl, a normal life, normal friends, and everything else. No one knows if I've ever been beaten, if I have an outraged stepfather, a drug-addicted mother, an alcoholic father, drug-dealing brothers, an unwanted sister. No one knows if I have all these things, but I do.

I stopped believing in happy endings a long time ago. I have never had a happy ending. I have cried oceans. Since I was four years old, I have been hit, shoved, slapped, punched, and thrown. You name it, I have been through it. CPS has been called more than once. But there have been so many memories. My earliest memory was when I was four years old and my mother made me sleep outside because her boyfriend did not want me in the house. So I slept outside in the middle of the summer being eaten up by mosquitoes.

Ever since I was born, everything was for him. If he did not want me around, I was not around. When he wanted someone to hit, I was the one he hit. He could not hit my brothers. They would either run away or try to hit him back, but I wouldn't. I would just sit there and take it. I would cry. Then my cries would turn into hysterics and my hysterics into screams, and my screams into cries again.

I do not have a perfect family. I don't even have a good, or normal, family. I have been forced to grow up way too fast. I have to do everything myself.

Karen has never had a normal life. She probably never will. She has never known the true love of a mother and father. She has never been cared for or protected. Her parents never told her she was smart or an outstanding leader. All over this country, kids have stories just like Karen's, or worse. They come to school after being exposed to these things every waking moment they are home. The teachers reprimand these kids for not bringing their pencils to class. How can a teacher read Karen's story and be angry because she did not have a pencil? Many teachers assume all their students have healthy home lives much like their own. They fail to enter their students' world. It may be because they are too busy, or it is "not their job" to get emotionally involved with their students. They say they teach math, science, English, social studies, etc., yet they fail to understand that they teach students. If a student does not know their teacher cares for them, why should they care about what that teacher has to say? They are on the receiving end of anger, yelling, and belittling at home. They do not need to come to school and suffer the same things at the hands of their teachers. As teachers, we may be the only "life preserver" some of these kids have.

As Karen continues her story, listen to the pain behind the words. She shares insights into the mind of a hopeless teenager. I am so thankful that Karen is no longer helpless, hopeless, or depressed. Does she have her ups and downs? Absolutely, she does. Who wouldn't?

> I don't ever remember my mother shedding a tear for me. It is ironic because I shed tears almost every night, but not anymore. Why should I waste tears on someone who has never cried for me? Yes, I have turned to drugs plenty of times, in an attempt to dull the pain. I have cut my own flesh so I could feel another type of pain. Cutting myself somehow made me feel better, but not anymore. No longer am I going to give myself scars just because my mother does not want to play her role as a parent. It hurts me inside, but I shouldn't let it get to me that bad. It's simply not worth it. I had to learn that the hard way.
>
> Who says I am not going to achieve something great? Why should I let my abusive stepfather ruin my life? Yet for a while, I thought I would never wake from this nightmare that was my life. I was just waiting for someone to hear my cries and shouts for help.

Luckily, I was awakened from this nightmare of a life by a very unlikely source. It was this old man that taught at our school. I had Coach Bridges' Teen Leadership class in eighth grade. But I first saw him while I was in seventh grade. I would be walking down the hall going to class, and Coach Bridges would be standing at his door between classes with this weird, goofy smile on his face, asking how our day was going. I told my friends he must be some kind of "freakin' idiot."

When I entered Teen Leadership in eighth grade, he would still smile and ask us how our day was going. *Like you'd care,* I used to think. *Why does my day matter to him? It's not affecting him, so why does he care?* Plus I was not about to tell some old guy the way my day was going. But there was something about him, something that moved me. It seemed like he actually cared, but why? What was so special about me? I was just a normal girl who got beat. But he did care. He did care that I cut myself. He did, he really did. I wondered what was so interesting about me. Could he tell that I cried myself to sleep last night? Could he see through the fake smile I put on every day to hide my pain? Could he see the pain behind my eyes? Obviously, he could. It was really clear to him. He saw through my smile and saw the pain. He could tell I cried myself to sleep because my eyes were puffy. Sometimes, I would even walk into his classroom crying. He would stop the class to make sure I was all right, and I wasn't … until then. I still question why, though. I am nothing special, but to him, I was special. I wouldn't be the person I am today if it wasn't for him.

How could I go on without Coach Bridges and my Teen Leadership classmates? When I came to the class, I had no self-motivation. I make A's and B's but do I hear anything at home like, "I'm proud of you"? No,

I haven't. So why try? Even though no one I know has done anything with their life doesn't mean I can't! I want to be a lawyer. I have heard plenty of times that I can't do something, or that I am too dumb. But you know what? I can do! Coach Bridges said I can! I can do whatever I want, and those people who tell me I can't are just jealous. Coach Bridges always said, "Let those things that have happened to you serve as stepping-stones towards your goal, and don't let anyone tear you down."

I am going to achieve something. I am going to follow my dreams. Even though they may seem unattainable right now, I am going to do it. I AM A LEADER. I can, and will, do something great with my life. I am going to DREAM BIG! I don't think I can. I <u>know</u> I can. Thanks, Coach!

Karen

Karen mentioned my telling her to let the negative things that have happened to her serve as stepping-stones to allow her to reach her goals and dreams. I learned this lesson during a hike in the mountains of northern New Mexico. Several years ago, I went on a "Men's getaway" with some friends. One of the friends owned a cabin on the side of a mountain. The area was teeming with trees and wildlife. One of the men actually saw a bear on one of his hikes. The bear was not close enough to pose a threat, but let's just say we were not exactly in the heart of a metropolis.

One day while I was hiking along a trail, I looked up the mountainside and saw a large rock formation jutting out from the top of a plateau. It reminded me of Pride Rock in the movie *The Lion King*. I knew if I could make it to the top of this formation the view would be absolutely breathtaking. The formation was about one hundred yards above me. My friend who owned the cabin told us about this rock formation. He said if I followed the trail for about one mile, the trail would wrap around and I would eventually reach this beautiful outlook. I do not know whether I was adventurous or just lazy, but I thought, *Why not just climb straight up the mountain? It can't be more than one hundred yards.*

The only problem was the fact that it was fairly steep and covered with bush-like trees about five to six feet tall. I began this little adventure and quickly realized that the soil was too loose to climb. My feet would slide out from under me with each step I took. At this rate, it would take me a couple of days to climb one hundred yards. For a moment, I thought about just taking the long trail, but then I decided to find a way to scale the mountain. It would be more difficult, but much less boring. Then it dawned on me! The small trees that I viewed as major obstacles to reaching my destination could serve as a means of reaching my destination.

As I began to climb, I would grip the limbs of these small trees (or large bushes) and pull myself up the mountain. Once I would make it past a tree, I would step on the trunk of the tree and use it as a stepping-stone to reach the next tree, which was no more than a few feet away. I methodically and patiently climbed from bush to bush until I reached my "Pride Rock." The view was more spectacular than I imagined. The climb was more than worth it! As I pondered the climb to this outlook, I realized that the very obstacles (bushes) that seemed to make the climb impossible to complete were the stepping-stones that allowed me to reach my destination.

We can allow the obstacles in our lives to lead to despair and hopelessness or we can consider them valuable tools that build within us the character and fortitude needed to reach our life dreams and goals. Anyone who lives a shallow life, sheltered from the possible dangers that may come their way, is not really living. How many people would pay money at the movie theater to watch a movie that has no conflict, no drama? The conflict is what makes the story. The difference between a tragic story and an inspirational story is how one responds to the conflicts of life.

I am dumbfounded by the resiliency these students have shown through their short lives. They seem to bounce back every time they are knocked down. They remind me of Rocky Balboa in the original

Rocky movie. Many of these students have been beaten to a pulp emotionally. Many of them will carry the scars of abuse for the rest of their lives. Yet carrying these scars can be a good thing. A scar is a sign of healing. If a student carries with them an emotional scar, it is no longer an open wound. The wound has healed.

I will never forget the first baseball game I played with metal spikes. I remember the excitement. All the players finally felt like real baseball players! The excitement lasted until the fourth inning. I was playing catcher with a runner on third base. The batter hit a hard ground ball to the shortstop, who threw it home to get the runner at the plate. The runner, who was good friend of mine, came in accidently with his spikes high. He spiked my left forearm at full speed. As I lay on the ground, I looked at my arm. The swelling had already started and blood was running down my arm onto the dirt. I left the game and Dad took me to the emergency room for X-rays to make sure my arm was not broken.

At the emergency room, the nurse first had to clean out the wound with no anesthetic. I would love to say I was courageous and took it like man. In actuality, I screamed like a girl. The X-rays were negative. The arm was not broken, but the scar is still fairly noticeable. It is interesting that as a look at my arm today and write this story, there is no more pain. I remember it hurt. I remember the tears. But that was the past. Now there is only a mark on my skin and a great story that becomes more dramatic with the telling. All scars have a story. Walk into any classroom, recreation center, or Boy Scout meeting and ask kids how they got their scars. We all love to tell the story of our scars. Girls try to hide them. Boys wear them like badges of honor. Scars symbolize courage and endurance. They remind us of a painful time in our lives, but they also remind us how we overcame that painful event and moved forward.

Scars can also serve as profound teachers. I have several scars, but I cannot think of any two scars I received in exactly the same way. After the spiking incident, I played baseball for six more years. I was never spiked again. Yes, a few runners slid under my tag, but I was never spiked. Many of my students carry emotional scars they will remember forever. Emotional scars can carry more pain than physical scars, but these courageous students have already made decisions to forgive, move forward, and stop the generational cycle of abuse to which their families have been held captive for decades.

Not all the students in my second-period class currently have an inspirational story. Some have turned away from "the road less traveled" and followed the highway leading to a dead end. It is the same highway their parents traveled. Some have parents who have struggled with drug addiction and have become addicted themselves at a very young age. As much as they hate what their parents' addictions have done to their family, they have followed the same path. But for the most part, these brave students have had the courage many adults never are able to muster. These students are brave enough to admit their mistakes and correct those mistakes. They have come to understand the definition of insanity: doing the same thing over and over, expecting different results. They know that acquiring different results requires a drastic departure from all that seems familiar to them. Very few ever demonstrate this depth of conviction. This is why the stories of this chapter are so moving. If these stories were common, they would not be so inspiring. This is why young ladies like Angela, Katrina, and Karen are going to impact the lives of thousands. I am glad I was fortunate enough to witness their transformation.

If this second-period class taught me anything, it taught me that life is not about the lemons life hands us but about what we do with those lemons. If we choose to make lemonade, the world will be a much better place. When we choose to use trials in our lives to make us stronger and more tenacious, we will not only change our own lives but we can effect entire generations to come. Even now, in the twenty-first century, lives have been molded and strengthened by the fortitude of the WWII generation. The enemies we fight today are different, but like my grandparents' generation, we can mold future generations by taking our lemons and making lemonade.

Chapter 4

A MEMORABLE EXPERIENCE

"A Memorable Experience" is the assigned topic for one of our speeches in our Teen Leadership class. This speech intrigued me because it was so wide open. My mind started racing through the list of possible experiences about which the kids could speak: a vacation to Disney World, a boy's dad taking him to his first Texas Rangers baseball game, someone's best Christmas ever, etc. This speech was going to be fun, and I anticipated it would be my favorite topic of the semester.

The students present this speech fairly early in the semester, so I do not have a great deal of time to prepare them to give professional speeches. But I knew the stories would be great. The first semester I taught Teen Leadership, I taught seventh graders. Most of my students were twelve and thirteen years old. The day I had been waiting for had finally arrived. I directed my students' attention to the whiteboard, where I posted a grading rubric for the speech, so they would know what I was watching for during their presentation. I sat at the back of the room in my director's chair and said with a loud voice, "Quiet on the set." I paused a few seconds until the talking stopped, and then I called out, "Action!"

The first student to give her speech was Tammy. Tammy was a very lively girl who always considered it a challenge to stay quiet and in her seat. So I knew it would be a speech to remember. I had no idea how right I would be.

She told us about a day in fifth grade, coming home from school. It was a day like any other day. She called out to her mother that she and her younger brother were home. There was no answer. She called out again, but still no answer. She walked down the hall and noticed the bathroom door was closed. She thought, *Oh, Mom's in the bathroom. That's why she did not hear me.* She called to her mom again as she knocked on the bathroom door.

"At that point, I began to get a little scared. I opened the bathroom door … I saw my mother's body. She had committed suicide." At this point, Tammy began to sob as she buried her face in her hands. Her best friend, who also knew Tammy's mother very well, approached Tammy and began to cry as well. The two girls held each other, crying, for a couple of minutes. I let them comfort each other for a moment. My Teen Leadership training did not prepare me to deal with this situation. I knew it was pivotal time for Tammy and the future of our class. I had to handle it with sensitivity and understanding. Yet I also needed to provide some leadership in order to help the class feel safe. I am sure none of the students had ever had a student talk about something so personal and so devastating at the same time.

After what seemed like an hour (probably two minutes at the most), I said to Tammy in a soft voice, "Sweetheart, you don't have to finish. You can sit down if you would like."

Tammy responded with strength and determination that shocked not only me but the whole class. "No, I want to finish, and I am going to finish." She continued to talk about the special relationship she had had with her mother and the depression she had dealt with for some time. At this point, most of the class was crying. Of course, the boys were trying to hide it well, but it was impossible to be in that room and not be touched by this demonstration of courage Tammy showed us.

As she concluded her speech, with chin held high and her shoulders drawn slightly back, she said, "I am proud of myself today, because I am standing her before you on my own two feet and

I refuse to let the loss of my mother ruin my life. I am going be somebody and I am going to make my mother proud."

Without my initiative or direction, the students spontaneously rose as one in a standing ovation! There was not a dry eye in the room, including my own. I had never been in a classroom like that before. These kids genuinely came together as a family that day. Our class would be forever changed. The depth of the relationships that grew out of that class was as strong as any class I ever had, or ever will have.

For years, I referred to Tammy as "Miss Teen Leadership." We shared a special bond. Even though my dad did not commit suicide, he lost a long battle with prostate cancer only months before. Sometimes, when there were a few minutes left in the class, Tammy and I would talk and share stories about our parents who were no longer with us. I learned a lot from Tammy. Her courage and zest for life in many ways encouraged me to go on and live my life in a way that would make my dad proud. I hope and pray that in some small way I have been able to do that.

It was at that time that I realized "A Memorable Experience" speeches were still going to be my favorite speech of the semester, but for much different reasons than I had thought. Over the next five years, I heard some absolutely horrific memorable experiences. I have had to call Child Protective Services six times, due to the content of my students' speeches. Fortunately, not all the speeches have been tragic. I have had a few funny speeches. One girl told us about the first time her parents let her stay home alone. She finished eating a snack and was putting her dishes in the sink. She panicked when she saw a lizard in the sink. She followed her parents' advice as to what to do in an emergency and promptly called 911. The 911 operator assured her she was in no danger. The police stopped by to check on her, but her parents were less than thrilled when they discovered how she handled the situation.

A couple of years later, I had a class (and a day) I will never forget. The speeches presented in this one class will always be engraved in my heart. I had two boxes of tissues in my room. Little did I know I would need both of them by the end of class.

Sherri told us about her family moving from Virginia to Texas. She said her mother had been depressed for a while before they moved. One day after returning home from school, she walked into her mother's bedroom and found her mother holding a gun to her own head about to commit suicide. Through tears and a cracking voice, she concluded her speech by describing how she had to talk her mother into putting the gun away. At eleven years old, Sherri was forced to be the protector and "guardian" of her own mother. Imagine the fear she must have faced knowing she was the only one standing between her mother and death. Finally, the tears turned to cries, which led to sobs. She was unable to finish her speech. We spent the next few minutes comforting her and assuring her we were there for her.

Later that day, I called CPS and reported what Sherri had said during her speech. CPS investigated immediately. Two days later, Sherri approached me while crying. She began screaming at me and cursing. She told me she hated me for reporting her and she would never speak to me again. I knew that was risk I had to take. I allowed her express her feelings toward me (colorful language included). Then we continued with our class. A week later, Sherri came to class with a smile on her face, thanking me for reporting her. She said her mother was now in counseling and was now getting the help she desperately needed.

This incident made me wonder how many stories like Sherri's never get reported. Fear closes the mouths of millions of children in this country every day. They are fearful of what might happen to them if they tell someone. They could be afraid they would be taken away from their parents. They could be afraid of what their parents might do to them if they revealed the "family secret." In the 1990s, there was a university study that concluded 94 percent of the things in life we worry about *never happen!* Many of the fears our children live with every day are unfounded. Granted, there is justification for many of them, but the fact remains that most of our "worry time" is spent on things that never happen.

Doug followed Sherri's speech. It was an extremely boring, noneventful speech. Although, it failed to capture the hearts of the class, it did serve to give us an opportunity to compose ourselves after Sherri's speech.

Adam presented the next speech. Adam was an African American student who was considered the jock of the school. In eighth grade, he already had the muscles of a sixteen- or seventeen-year-old. He was the strongest and fastest athlete in our school. He was full of energy and life. He was a class clown and never sat still for longer than about three minutes. He had a very loud, high-pitched voice that did not match his muscular build at all. His voice was similar to that of Mike Tyson.

Adam began his speech speaking about his wonderful mother. It was easy to see in his eyes the admiration he held for his mother. He told us his mother was a single mother. Adam's father had been in prison since Adam was born. His mother did her best to give Adam the love and attention he needed while attempting to hold down two, sometimes three, jobs at once, just to provide for the family. On her days off, she would take Adam bowling or they spent hours playing at the park. She had a gift for making any occasion, no matter how meager the resources, into a major, unforgettable event. Adam's love for his mother coated every word of his speech.

As Adam continued, he told the class he began to notice his mother was not feeling well, and they stopped going to the park. He kept asking her if she was all right. Smiling, his mother would always say she was just tired. Finally, her pain grew to be too much. She could no longer keep the news from him. One day, when Adam came home from kindergarten, his grandfather met him at the bus stop. His grandfather walked him home. When they entered the front door, Adam saw his mother and grandmother sitting on the couch. He noticed both of them had been crying.

"Baby, come sit over here by me. Mommy has something to tell you." Adam slowly walked across the room and sat between his mother and grandmother. He did not understand what was going on, but he did know it was not good news his mother needed to tell him.

"Sweetheart," she said, placing her arm around Adam, "I am very, very sick. The doctors say I have cancer."

Adam was not sure what cancer was, but he did know he never saw anyone speak about cancer with a smile on his or her face. "Can they give you medicine, Mommy?" Adam asked.

"Yes, sweetie, but the medicine could make me sick also. It will take a long time for Mommy to start feeling good again," his mother answered while failing to hold back the tears.

As Adam continued his speech, he told us that the treatments his mother underwent seemed to help for a while. His mother started smiling again. They started having picnics at the park again. But after several months, the cancer returned with a vengeance. One morning, Adam woke up late for school. He walked through the house looking for his mother. He began walking back to his mother's bedroom. He assumed she'd slept through the alarm. He walked into the bedroom and saw his mom in bed like he thought he would. Only, when he tried to wake her there was no response.

He began screaming, "Mommy, Mommy, wake up! Wake up!" But there was still no response. His mother's long battle with cancer had come to an end.

As Adam told the class his mother had passed away, he covered his face with his hands and began sobbing uncontrollably. Here he was—the guy who was the toughest kid in the school was uncontrollably and unashamedly crying in front of his friends. No one at the middle school had ever seen him cry. At first, no one knew what to do. Then another boy in the class and two girls slowly approached Adam. With tears running down their own cheeks, the three students embraced Adam in large group hug. When the rest of the class saw Adam respond favorably to his friends, the rest of the class joined in the hug.

I sat back in awe of how these wonderful students, who had been through so much, rallied around their friend. I could have watched that scene all day.

After the class returned to their seats, five other students gave their speeches about the police breaking down their front doors to arrest their fathers. One of the greatest and most common challenges my students have faced over the last five years is finding it within themselves to forgive their fathers. Many of my students have had fathers who have been abusive, drug addicted, neglectful, absent, alcoholic, imprisoned, etc. Many of them have learned, over time, to forgive their fathers. Others readily admit they know they must forgive but are presently unable to take that step. I explained to them sometimes a person has to forgive "as much as they are able at the present time."

At the end of the class period, on speech days, the students are given the opportunity to tell other students in the class what they enjoyed about their speeches. It builds the confidence of those receiving the encouragement, but it also helps those encouraging others to communicate positive words of encouragement without embarrassment or feeling self-conscious. Giving positive feedback is usually much easier for the girls, in that girls are generally much more relational than boys.

After several students shared, it was evident the comments were coming to an end. Just as I was preparing conclude the feedback session, Doug raised his hand. The reader may recall Doug was the student who had given a less-than-earth-shattering speech earlier in the class. Doug was also a very good athlete who consistently gave the impression he was "too cool for school."

"I really respect all you guys who shared all that personal stuff. That took a lot of guts," Doug stated. He then looked at me and asked in a very humble voice which seemed foreign to him, "Coach Bridges, could I redo my speech?"

I nodded and Doug stepped to the front of the room.

I transferred here last year from Alabama. I have moved a lot, so I don't usually tell people much about my personal life. But y'all showed me that it's okay to talk about your personal life in here. My most memorable experience was not unlike many of yours. The only difference is I remember the cops kicking down my door to arrest my mother.

My mother and I were home. It was a hot summer day. We heard a loud knock at the door. "Open up! It's the police!" I heard a cop yell from the front porch. My mom yelled some cuss words and ran out the back door. The cops broke down the door and started chasing my mom out the back door. By the time they got outside, my mom had already jumped on an ATV and was riding away. The cops were running after her with their guns drawn. My mom was so scared she ran the ATV through a barbed-wire fence. My mom flipped off the ATV and landed on part of the fence, cutting her neck. She ran into the woods with her neck bleeding and the cops hot on her heels.

I was only ten years old, so I didn't know what to do. I just curled up in the corner of the living room and started crying. I was still crying an hour later when my big brother got home. He asked me why I was crying. When I told him what happened, he beat me up for letting the cops take my mom.

Although his chin quivered as he finished the story, he never shed a tear. Even though he opened up about his personal life for the first time, he still could not allow himself to show any weakness. He then quietly walked to his seat. We all sat in silence for a few seconds until the bell rang. For the first time all semester, the entire class left the room in silence.

The next day, we continued the speeches. We had already heard several speeches that were somewhat overwhelming. Even though some of the speeches were difficult to listen to, the raw emotion of the speeches drew the entire class closer. It helped us truly become a family.

We had one student, a wonderful young lady named Alyssa, tearfully share with us her battle with anorexia. She explained how she had battled it and what she thought was the cause: a stepfather who kept calling her fat. (And she was far from it.) She also learned in Teen Leadership what to do with comments like the ones made to her by her stepfather. As the semester continued, she was able to help other girls in the class who had been leaning toward an anorexic lifestyle. Had she not had the courage to speak up about her eating disorder, those girls may not have found the help they needed.

Alyssa's courage gave Amber courage to share her story. Amber's story took the family atmosphere of our class to whole new level.

"Last summer I got to spend a week in California with some relatives who live there." I remember breathing a sigh of relief. Amber was actually going to give a speech about a happy, fun-filled California vacation. This was more like it! Amber continued,

> When I arrived, my aunt and uncle welcomed me with open arms. They had not seen me for three years so they could not believe how I had grown. My uncle said, "You don't look like a little girl anymore. You look like a young lady." After I unpacked, we all went to the beach and had a great time. It had been a long flight to California, so by the time bedtime rolled around I was exhausted.
>
> I went to bed about 11:00 p.m. and fell fast asleep. I woke up at 2:00 a.m. with my uncle in bed with me, touching me.

Amber was unable to continue her speech. She burst into tears. Two girls rushed to her aid and helped her back to her seat. I felt like I was about to vomit. Amber was one of the sweetest girls I ever had the privilege of teaching. How could someone do something like that? It literally made me sick. In a soft voice, I addressed the class. I knew none of them had ever heard anyone tell an entire class something so personal and so painful.

"We are not going to have any more speeches today, and I think you understand why. Amber just showed a great deal of courage in sharing that story with us. It says a lot about her courage and her character. But it also says something about you as her classmates. She would not have shared what she did if she was not convinced it was safe to do so. Having said that, I need all eyes on me for just a moment."

Everyone looked my way except Amber and two girls who were consoling her.

"What Amber shared today was *extremely* personal. We have always stressed confidentiality in this class. It is times like this that we must practice it. If I find out anyone in this room has shared what Amber just shared with us, outside the walls of this room, I will personally do whatever I can to have you removed from this class permanently. Is that understood?"

The entire class nodded in agreement. To this day, I have yet to hear *any* rumors of anyone in the class gossiping about what Amber shared. In fact, I have never received word of anyone breaking a confidence in the eight years I have taught Teen Leadership.

Afterward, I spoke privately with Amber. After applauding her courage in sharing about the incident with her uncle, I asked her if she had ever told anyone about what happened. She told me she had not. She had not even told her mother. When I asked her what compelled her to tell the whole class what happened, she simply responded, "This is the first place I felt safe enough to share it." If only all the classrooms across America could be so safe.

At the end of our conversation, I explained to Amber that I would have to call Child Protective Services (CPS). She understood. She went home that day and told her mother what happened. They contacted the authorities and her uncle is now serving time in prison. A few days later, Amber thanked me for reporting the incident. She said it felt like the world was lifted off her shoulders. Her life was forever changed for the better because a classroom full of students decided to live by a social contract and become a family.

In fact, as the semester progressed, the walls that are so apparent in most classrooms continued to fall. By Christmas break, we were speaking freely in our "family time" and students were helping other students who had similar struggles they had once faced. The last assignment I give my classes is to write me a letter. Many of them described the class as a class like no other they ever had. They felt like our class was like a sanctuary, an oasis, of sorts. They could come to our class and know they would be loved and accepted for who they were. There was no need to wear a mask. And if someone did wear a mask, someone else would call him or her on it. We gave each other permission to speak into our lives. It was not always pretty, but I have witnessed thirteen- and fourteen-year-olds deal with conflicts in front of the entire class in a much healthier manner than most adults I know.

The last day of class, before we left for our Christmas break, we had a party. We had been through too much together not to celebrate what we had experienced and accomplished. We laughed, told jokes, and reminisced about the semester. Yet when we looked at the clock and knew we had only a few minutes together as a Teen Leadership class, the tears began to flow. Yes, even some of the boys were crying. There was a "knowing," deep down inside all of us, that we had experienced something very special, something so special we may never experience it again.

These "Memorable Experience" speeches over the years have served as glue that held our classes together. As the students shared their stories, they realized they were not alone. Other students had been through very similar experiences as they had. These speeches were the tools used to build bridges between students who, otherwise, would never have communicated, much less become friends.

In our individualistic society today, with our rear-entry garages, privacy fences, gated communities, cell phones, and social networking, I wonder if we would not do ourselves a favor by intentionally spending some extended face-to-face time with our friends and family. When I grew up, we ate family dinner together every night. We would not miss it. If we missed it, we just did not eat. Today, when I ask my students how many of them sit down together with the family for dinner, the average affirmative response is between 5 and 10 percent. Yes, our schedules are much busier than our grandparents' were, so we need to be even more intentional about the time we do spend together.

There was once a college professor who wanted to illustrate a lesson for his students. He stood behind his lectern as he slowly scanned the room. His eyes told the students, "Watch, and be amazed." From behind the lectern, he revealed a large glass jar. He then reached under the lectern and set four large rocks down on the table adjacent to the lectern. He proceeded to carefully place the large rocks in the glass jar. The final rock was flush with the brim of the jar.

"Is this jar full?" A dull roar could be heard from the students as they debated among themselves whether or not the jar was full. About two-thirds of the class said no, and one-third said yes.

Then from behind the lectern, the professor removed a large bag full of gravel. He began to slowly pour the gravel into the jar. The gravel trickled down over the large rocks, filling in the empty space of the jar left by the large rocks. When he had filled the jar to the brim with gravel, the professor asked the same question.

"Is the jar full now? The students were beginning to see where the professor was logically going with this illustration. A few more students chimed in with those who said the jar was not full.

The professor then sat a small bucket of sand on the table. He began, with great care, to pour the sand into the jar. The sand filled in the empty space between the pebbles of gravel. It took much longer to fill the jar to the brim with sand. Not unlike watching an hourglass, the students were growing somewhat impatient. They already knew where he was going with this exercise, or so they thought.

One last time, the professor asked, "Is the jar full *now?*" This time, more students were of the opinion that the jar was indeed now full. The professor continued smiling while no less than a dozen small conversations began all across the room. Nervous laughter, along with *oooohhhs* and *aaaaahhhs*, could be heard as the professor set a pitcher of water on the table. The professor carefully poured the water from the pitcher into the jar. If he poured too fast, the water would spill over the brim and onto the table. Yet as he slowly poured, the water began to soak the sand and fill in any and all empty spaces between the grains of sand. He poured the entire pitcher of water into the jar.

"What is the main point of this object lesson?" asked the professor.

After a moment, of awkward silence, some opinions were offered.

"Where there's a will, there's away."

"No matter how busy you are, you can still fit more in your schedule!" They were after all, college students.

"The term *full* is a relative term!" shouted one student in the back of the room.

The professor, after taking into consideration all of the answers, proceeded to respond. "While all the proposed answers have an element of truth to them, none of them are the main point of the lesson. Actually, the main point of this object lesson is quite simple. If one wants to fill the jar with all these substances, they have to put the big rocks in first."

If one truly desires to build a family atmosphere, whether it is in one's own home or in their classroom, one question cries out for an answer: what are your big rocks? For many, God, or their faith, would be their first rock. Almost everyone would include, in one form or another, family or relationships as one of their rocks. So if we truly value relationships, we are going to nurture and cultivate those relationships. One of the most effective ways to do this is to recover the forgotten art of listening. As parents and/or teachers, we need to take time to listen to our kids, whether they are our children or our students. As the cute little kids turn into teenagers, the need for good listening skills grows even more. This is a challenge seeing that most adults would rather avoid any and all conversations with teenagers.

I once attended a workshop for teachers. The speaker was a district superintendent for a school district in south Texas. He had very humorous quote. "There is no problem your middle school student may have that a little reasoning won't make worse." While this is true, in many instances, keep in mind that one can listen to teenagers without reasoning with them. I have had students come to me with problems that have been solved simply by my listening to them. The more they talked, the more they recognized the source of the problem. They would leave my room thanking me for my help, when I never said a word. Sometimes, a kid just needs to know an adult cares about them enough to listen.

The best role model I had in regards to building and sustaining relationships was my father. My dad was, and still is, my hero. He passed away from prostate cancer in 2004. A few weeks before his death, he and I were having a conversation about the important things in life. I believe his reflections are worth noting here.

> David, since I have had cancer, I noticed that the grass has never been greener and the sky has never been bluer. I realize now how many small blessings I have always just taken for granted. It is important to stop and smell the roses, but through my sickness, the one thing God has made clear to me, like never before, is that the only thing eternal in this life is people.

During my years in church ministry, I did over a hundred funerals. I have been at the deathbed of many of them. Not once did I hear a man say, "David, my only regret is that I didn't spend more time at the office."

While we, as teachers, must teach our students the core content of our classes, we must always remember that we first and foremost *teach students.*

Chapter 5

UNITY THROUGH DIVERSITY

One of the factors that make Teen Leadership such an awesome class is the diversity represented in each class. In setting schedules for the students, we attempt to have a good cross-section of the student body represented in each class. Before we begin this chapter in earnest, please understand that any references to race, religion, and the like are not in any way to show prejudice or favoritism for one group over another. The author is simply identifying the differences in order to show it is possible for different races, religions, and political affiliations to respect one another and actually work together. Throughout my experience teaching Teen Leadership, I have found that kids are much better at it than are adults.

The first year I taught Teen Leadership on class in particular had a very diverse and interesting group of characters. I noticed when I checked roll I had a difficult time pronouncing several of the names. I also noticed there were several different races represented. One of the goals of Teen Leadership is to teach students how to work with people from different backgrounds, with different cultural values and belief systems. As I looked around the room, I thought, *If they don't learn these things in this class, they never will.* My job as their teacher was to build a family atmosphere with twenty-two students from eight different countries and five different races. I faintly heard the theme song from *Mission Impossible* in the back of my mind.

Never being one to shy away from a challenge, I enthusiastically jumped in the deep pool of diversity with both feet. We played several games during the first week to get to know each other better. I quickly learned that we had students from the USA, Mexico, Guatemala, Honduras, Lithuania, Jordan, Thailand, and South Korea. During our family times, we would have an opportunity to ask students questions about their homeland and what it was like growing up in a different country. The eagerness of the students to learn about their friends' cultures was a very encouraging sign that we could grow this class of twenty-two students into a family.

While the students were presenting their "Memorable Experience" speeches, a young man from Lithuania stood to give his speech. He prefaced his speech by telling us he did not actually remember the experience he was about to tell us about. He was only three years old at the time, but his father told him about the story.

This young man (we will call him David) and his family lived in Bosnia during the war. One day he was playing just outside his house. There were flowers in a field not far from his house so he decided to go investigate what made such beautiful colors. Being three years old, he did not think to ask his parents' permission, nor was he aware that he lived in a war zone. He wanted to pick some flowers for his mother. Just as he picked the first flower, he heard his mother scream, "David, don't move!" She then began to scream for David's father to come quickly. David's father ran around the corner only to see his three-year-old son standing in the middle of a minefield. He was about seventy-five yards away from his father. His father slowly and carefully walked ever so softly toward David. David's father told him they were going to play a game. "David, I am going to walk to you very slowly. To win the game you have to be completely still until I touch you. If you stay still until I touch you, you win the game and I will give you a prize." David's father finally reached him and he never moved. David won the game … and lived.

Throughout the semester, the students would give speeches that would often refer to their home countries. It almost became a Teen

Leadership/geography/sociology class. The students gained a great deal more insight than simply how to give speeches. They learned about cultures, leadership, and how to work with those who maintain a very different worldview. For some of the students, English was their second language, so the speeches helped them gain confidence in their English as well as overcoming their fear of speaking English before a large group.

Although the diversity in this class was greatest of any class I have ever taught, it was also one of the most rewarding. The very things that caused some of these students to judge others who were different subsequently drew the class together. While this was the most diverse class I ever taught, it definitely was not the only diverse class. In fact, I have had students much different from me in every class.

In the last chapter, I told you about Adam, who lost his mother to cancer. Adam and I became extremely close. He had no father at home so I hoped, in some small way, to fill that void the best I could. I would make sure he was doing his homework in his other classes and that he was behaving in the classroom as well. It was interesting how close we had become. Here I was a gray-haired, white teacher and coach. I grew up in a middle class family. My dad saved every penny he could to send me to a private high school and later a private university. One could say I was spoiled as a child and I would find it difficult to argue with them. Then there was Adam, a poor African American student being raised by his grandparents. His mother had passed away from cancer and his dad had been in prison his whole life. We did not have much in common, but that did not keep us from loving each other and respecting each other. If I have learned one thing while teaching Teen Leadership, I have learned that love and respect are choices. They are not emotions. Tina Turner calls love "a second-hand emotion." I call it the greatest force the world has ever known. One of my mentors, Jimmy Seibert, once said, "Anything is possible when you fear nothing and are in love."

Another young man in my class I grew to love was Razzaq. Razzaq was from Jordan. He had moved with his father to the United States a year before attending my class. Obviously, moving to America was quite a culture shock for Razzaq. When he arrived in the United States, he knew virtually no English. His father taught him English and worked extremely well with his teachers. His father called me one day and asked if I could send home any written work Razzaq turned in so he could help Razzaq with his writing at home. Actually, by the time Razzaq arrived in my class, he possessed an outstanding working knowledge of the English language. I was shocked that he had only been studying English for a year. This was a credit to both Razzaq's intelligence and his father's dedication to give him the tools he would need to be successful.

Although Razzaq was doing well in his English studies, there were other areas where he struggled. I have had the opportunity to visit nine different countries, and one thing I have learned is that kids are kids, no matter where they live. So let us just say that Razzaq sometimes had difficulty behaving in class. He loved to talk and many times disrupted the class. This was not his only problem. He also struggled with his social skills. Razzaq had to face bullying and teasing. Some of it was very mean spirited because of his ethnic and religious background. I made it quite clear that none of that would be tolerated in my classroom, and for the most part, the students treated him very well. But Razzaq would confide in me at times about instances he would face outside of my classroom. Yet overall, he maintained a positive attitude and grew very close. We would talk often about the Jordanian football team. Razzaq loved soccer. His dream was to one day return to Jordan and play for the national team.

One of the major differences between Razzaq and me was our religious views. He was raised in very strict Muslim family with solid and unwavering traditions. Razzaq would faithfully observe Ramadan with his family. During Ramadan, Muslims fast during the daylight hours for one month. Razzaq attended my class just before lunch. So at the end of the class each day, I would escort the class to the cafeteria. Razzaq would continue on to the office and spend the lunch period there so he would not have to be around everyone else eating food in front of him. He never wavered and never complained. He always stayed true to his convictions.

An important piece of the Teen Leadership curriculum is the personal stories the teacher tells regarding the particular lesson being studied that day. As a result, many of my personal stories centered around my experiences as a youth pastor and pastor for several years, along with the countless hours I spent counseling young people. Let me state here that I fully respect the laws concerning the so-called "separation of church and state." I have never proselytized any of my students. After sharing a story focusing on empathy and listening skills, I told a story about a hospital visit I made to a woman who was about to die of cancer. It is a very powerful story and my students were hanging on every word. After class I was escorting my students to the cafeteria for lunch. As usual, Razzaq was walking with me. Every day we would have these five-minute talks on the way to the cafeteria.

As we walked to the cafeteria that day Razzaq asked me a question. "Coach Bridges, I think you are most caring man I have ever met. I want to be a teacher like you when I grow up. You are a Christian, right?"

"Well, you could say that I am a follower of Issa." Issa is the name given to Jesus in the Quran. I know that for many Muslims, the word *Christian* conjures up visions of the Crusades and other conflicts throughout history Christians have perpetrated against Muslims. I did not want Razzaq to identify me with anything like that.

I could tell my answer intrigued Razzaq.

"Coach, can you tell me about Christianity?" As much as I wanted to, I knew it was not my place. So I gave Razzaq a piece of paper with my cell phone number.

"Razzaq, give this number to your father and ask him to call me. I will explain the conversation we had today and answer any questions he may have. Tell him I would even be willing to come to your home and all three of us could discuss your questions together."

Razzaq agreed. The next day, Razzaq shook my hand at the door. "I gave my father your number and told him about our conversation. He told me he would tell me about Christianity." I completely understood, but there was a respect that was formed with that experience, not only between Razzaq and me but also between Razzaq's father and me. I did not discover the impact it had on Razzaq's father until a few weeks later, but that story is for a later chapter. Over the next several weeks, Razzaq and I grew closer and he began showing marked improvement in his grades, not only in my class but in other classes as well.

Razzaq and I grew up in different countries, different cultures, and different religions. Society would tell us we have nothing in common and therefore have no basis for a relationship, and some would actually expect us to be enemies. Yet at the end of semester, Razzaq told me I was the best teacher he ever had, and thanks to me he wanted to be a teacher. Teachers are not supposed to have favorites, but if I did, Razzaq would be close to the top of the list. It is possible to be different and still respect the views of others. This does not mean you have to agree with them, but you can still respect them.

A perfect example of this would be my relationship with a girl named Jennifer. I could tell from the very first day of school that Jennifer was a disturbed young lady. There was a great deal of anger in her eyes. She dressed like most "Goths" in all black, along with the classic black fingernail polish and lipstick complement the ensemble. She loved to wear black band shirts, which would not be bad, but the names of the bands and logos were quite disturbing. Several of the bands and the logos seemed to have certain connections with the occult.

One day in an attempt to reach out to Jennifer, I asked her, "Jennifer, who is your favorite band?"

"Murder Dolls," she said without a hesitation.

"Murder Dolls?" I asked, hoping I misunderstood her.

"Yes. Murder Dolls."

"As in little Raggedy Ann dolls that murder people?" I was hoping she would see where I was headed with my questioning.

"Yeah, I guess."

"Tell me, Jennifer, what do you like about this Murder Dolls band?"

"I like the music. It's cool," she said proudly.

"Hey, when I was a teenager, I used that line too. I told my parents I didn't listen to the lyrics. I just liked the music. It's funny, though, how I had every song memorized."

Jennifer rolled her eyes.

I continued. "I also hated it when adults would judge both me and my music without even listening to it."

Jennifer interrupted, "Yeah, I hate that too! What's that about?"

"I don't know. But I tell you what. I'll give you the benefit of the doubt. I am not going to judge this Murder Dolls group of yours, but I would like you to bring your Murder Dolls CD to class tomorrow, along with the case."

"Why? Are you going to take it up or something?" Jennifer asked suspiciously.

"No. I just want to read the lyrics, because I don't want to judge something without investigating it first."

"That's cool. I'll bring it tomorrow," Jennifer said emphatically.

The next day, Jennifer came in the room with a big smile on her face, CD in hand. "Here you go, Coach."

I thanked her.

While the class was working on a small group assignment, I decided to read the lyrics of CD. After reading a few songs, I did not know whether to laugh, cry, or throw up. I had no idea it was legal to sell CDs like this in our country. One song in particular caught my eye. The title of the song was "Grave Robbers U.S.A." (a song dedicated to necrophilia). This was a thirteen-year-old girl listening to this refuse.

I called Jennifer up to my desk. While she approached my desk, my eyes stayed glued to the lyrics on the CD sleeve. I could see out of the corner of my eye Jennifer's sheepish look on her face.

"Yes, sir?" she asked shyly, which was not like her at all.

"So is this what you want to do when you grow up?"

"What?"

"Dig up dead bodies and have sex with them?" My eyes continued to stay fixed on the lyrics.

"No! That's gross!"

"So why do you listen to it?"

"I like the music," Jennifer answered defensively.

"There is probably a lot of music that sounds like them that does not tell kids that necrophilia is cool."

"Well …" Jennifer had no response.

The next portion of our conversation concerned me even more. I turned to the front cover of the CD. Sure enough, there was a blue and yellow NC-17 warning label.

"Jennifer, do you see this sticker on the CD?"

"Yeah," she replied.

"This means that you should not purchase this or listen to it if you are under seventeen years old." I was actually thinking no one should ever be listening to it. "Does your mother know you listen to this stuff?"

"Yeah, she bought it for me." I wanted to scream. What parent in their right mind would buy something like this for their thirteen-year-old daughter to listen to?

"Your mom bought this for you?"

"Yeah," she responded, with a hint of embarrassment in her voice.

"Is this your mom's favorite group too?" I asked. One would think this would be a rhetorical question, but now it seemed to be an honest question that demanded an answer.

"No, her favorite band is Korn." At this point, I felt like I needed to go to extremes to make a point. Luckily, I had done some research on Korn a few years previously.

So I asked Jennifer, "What is your mom's favorite Korn song?"

"I don't know."

"Is it the song that only has two words in the lyrics, one of them being the 'F' word?"

Jennifer had a shocked look on her face. There were some other songs I asked her about that had lyrics I would rather not repeat in this book. She was not shocked at the lyrics I was explaining to her. She was shocked that I knew about the lyrics. I told Jennifer I was not angry with her, but I was deeply troubled and concerned for her. She nodded as if to say, "I understand." Although it was a difficult conversation to have with Jennifer, that conversation set the stage for a deeper, more meaningful relationship between us.

A couple of weeks later, I was monitoring the lobby area of the school before the first bell. There were about two hundred students sitting along the walls of the lobby while waiting for school to begin. As I would walk around the lobby, it was not uncommon for me to stop for a moment and interact with some of the students. I always try to be happy and cheerful, especially early in the morning. I walked past Jennifer and she called my name to get my attention. I turned and noticed she had a small whiteboard similar to the whiteboards in our classrooms. This one, however, was small. The students would often use these boards in their math classes.

"Hey, Mr. Bridges, I have some of the lyrics to one of my favorite songs! You want to read them?" Jennifer's voice was sincere, but something about her facial expression told me to prepare myself. The lyrics seemed very cryptic and mysterious. I could not make out what the writer was trying to say until I read the last line: "For I love to embrace your witchcraft." When I read those lyrics, my heart sank. The last line confirmed what I had already suspected. I lowered the whiteboard just enough for Jennifer to see my eyes.

With raised eyebrows, I asked, "So you're a witch?" Actually, it was more of a statement than a question. Jennifer quickly looked around to see if anyone else heard. She leaned forward as if to tell me to lower my voice, although I said it very quietly.

"How did you know?" asked Jennifer.

"Well, the last line was a small clue, but I had suspected it for some time." I reminded Jennifer that I was in church ministry for twenty-two years and that I probably knew more about witchcraft than she did. I also warned her how dangerous it was and I let her know emphatically that I was very concerned for her well-being.

Jennifer defensively replied, "I'm not a bad witch. I'm a white witch. I cast spells to help people, not hurt them. It's not like I'm a Devil worshipper or anything."

"Yeah, but he's the source of all of it," I said.

"Yeah, but—"

I quickly interrupted her because I did not want this very important point to go unnoticed. "Wait right there. See, you just admitted the Devil's the source of it, so don't try to cover it up with your spiritual lingo."

Jennifer looked at the floor, somewhat at a loss for words. I stooped down so I could be more on her level, as she was sitting on the floor. My body language and my tone of voice softened considerably. "Jennifer, let me ask you a question. What if the drug cartel in Bogotá, Colombia, gave a million dollars to the Hurricane Katrina relief effort? That would be a good thing, wouldn't it?"

"Yeah, I guess."

"Does that make the drug cartel a good thing?"

Jennifer looked away, pondering how to answer. Before she had a chance to answer, I stood up and slowly walked away. I knew an extended debate with her would cause her to be defensive and dig in her heels. I wanted to leave her with something to think about, so she could save face (and respect) but still consider the seriousness of her actions.

Our conversation must have had some impact on her. The very next day, as I stood at the door shaking hands with my students as they entered my room, I saw Jennifer walking toward me with a big smile. I returned the smile and held out my hand to greet her. I noticed something different about her (besides her smile). It only took me a few seconds to realize what was different. She had black eyeliner, black lipstick, black fingernail polish, black shoes, black pants, a black hoodie, and a *baby blue T-shirt*. I wanted her to know I noticed, but I did not want to cause a scene or draw too much attention to her. I was afraid it would scare her into wearing all black again.

"Jennifer, I love your shirt. It looks very nice on you," I said with a smile.

With the grin of a toddler on Christmas morning, Jennifer replied, "Thanks, Mr. Bridges. I wore it just for you!" That was better than any present she could have given me. That was a huge step for her. The funny thing is, no one else even noticed.

Our relationship continued to grow over the next several weeks. I tried to plant a few seeds where I could. Jennifer began to smile more and interact with other students in a much more positive manner. Not only that her grades were improving as well. Things were going quite smoothly for Jennifer, at least in my class. That is until what I lovingly refer to as "The Jerry Smackdown."

Jerry was one of the students in Jennifer's class. Jerry and Jennifer probably could not be more different. Jennifer was a Latina student from a broken home and by all appearances was pretty tough. Many of the girls in the school were afraid of her. Jerry, on the other hand, had a fair complexion with freckles and blond hair that was almost white. He grew up in a very stable middle class family and was extremely close to his dad. I even think Jerry was a little smaller than Jennifer as well. I will never forget my first exposure to Jerry's world. The first week of class, I had the students complete a student profile so I could get to know them better. I asked many questions about their likes and dislikes, their hobbies and their families. The final question simply gave them an opportunity to tell me anything else they thought would be good for me to know. Jerry wrote in all capital letters, "I HAVE AN A+ AVERAGE AND I'M A BAPTIST!!!" I thought, *This kid should be interesting, to say the least.*

How right I was. We have all heard the phrase opposites attract. This definitely was not the case for Jennifer and Jerry.

Throughout the semester, I would hear little verbal barbs exchanged between Jerry and Jennifer and three or four of Jennifer's Goth friends, but nothing too serious. Then one day, we had a lesson on "image." In this lesson, we discussed our self-image and did some activities to see if the image the students presented in public was consistent with the image they *wanted* to present. This led to a discussion about fashion and how the clothes we wear can be an important part of that image.

That was the chance Jerry had been waiting for. He was not going to let this opportunity pass him by. He went on a verbal rampage attacking Jennifer and her friends.

"What kind of image are you guys trying to present dressing in all black every day, with your black lipstick? Are you trying to look like you're dead or something? What is that about? That's just stupid!"

At first, I felt the need to correct Jerry for his disrespectful behavior, but I thought Jennifer and her friends could handle it. Not to mention our social contract stated that when there was a conflict, we needed to talk it out. So I decided to give them an opportunity to follow the social contract. Jennifer calmly told Jerry that they liked to wear black and could not understand why it was any of his business how they dressed.

Jerry continued his assault on Jennifer and her friends, and it was on! They went back and forth for about ten minutes. It became very heated, with Jerry and Jennifer and her friends all standing. Luckily, they sat across the room from each other so there was no danger of physical violence. In the midst of the argument, a very sweet, shy girl in the class raised her hand.

"Yes?" I asked. I was excited because she never said anything in class. I was waiting for these great words of wisdom that would end the conflict instantly, leaving both parties at a loss for words! The students became silent in anticipation. The girl then nervously swallowed before she spoke. "Can I leave the room? I am starting to feel uncomfortable."

With a comforting smile, I urged her to stay so we could all see this through. If these kids could resolve this conflict, they could resolve any conflict.

For the most part, Jerry stayed on the offensive, quoting Scriptures from the Bible and predicting where the other girls would spend eternity after they died. Actually, he was quite judgmental and arrogant. Yet Jennifer and her friends never became defensive. They respected Jerry even though they disagreed with almost everything he was saying. They stayed focused on the issue at hand and never resorted to personal attacks.

As the discussion was drawing to a close, Jerry's anger was rapidly escalating. Jerry made some comment about their witchcraft and obsession with vampires.

Finally, Jennifer had enough. She retorted, "Look, you don't have agree with how live or how we dress or anything else about us, but you still have to respect us!"

"I'm not going to respect any Devil worshippers!"

The spontaneous *oooohhhs* of the other students filled the room. Jennifer waited until everyone was quiet again and gained her composure. Pointing at me, Jennifer responded. "There is no one in this school that disagrees more with my lifestyle than Mr. Bridges. And no one respects me more than him either."

I was shocked. Her response totally surprised me. With that, Jerry shrugged his shoulders, rolled his eyes, and sat down. It seemed both parties agreed to disagree. I explained to them that there was nothing wrong with that.

"You are not always going to agree with everyone, but you can *choose* to respect everyone. My respecting others has nothing to do with them and everything to do with me. I respect people because that is who I am. Where would the world be if everyone waited until someone *earned* their respect before respect was given? We would all be waiting around disrespecting each other. What kind of world would that be?"

With that, the bell sounded. It brought a whole new meaning to the phrase *saved by the bell*. As the students left the room, I asked Jerry to stay for a moment.

"Jerry, you know I am a Christian, right?"

"Yes, sir," Jerry responded proudly, waiting for a pat on the back.

"Jerry, when people ask me if I am a Christian, I tell them that I am a follower of Jesus. The reason I say that is because when many people think of Christians, they think of scenes like the one they just witnessed in here."

"What do you mean?" Jerry asked.

"I agreed with many of the things you said. You stated many things that were 'true.' But the hurtful way you presented those truths negated them. Jesus never talked that way to 'sinners.' The only people Jesus confronted because of their attitudes and actions were the religious people."

Jerry lowered his head. It was obvious he was embarrassed.

"Sorry, Mr. Bridges," Jerry mumbled.

"Hey, Jerry, you don't have to apologize to me. You didn't say anything hurtful to me."

Jerry simply gave a knowing nod of his head. The next day, he apologized to Jennifer and her friends for how he acted. In the end, the "Jerry Smackdown" brought our class closer than it had ever been. Jerry was a good kid. He did not mean to be hurtful. He was simply trying to stand up for what he believed. He just allowed his zeal to overcome his wisdom. Rumors about the "Jerry Smackdown" traveled all over the school by the end of the day. At least for a few days, our class was famous. The kids learned that families have conflicts. Devoted families work through them and continue to love each other. It would be wonderful if someone could invent a way to teach adults that lesson.

Just because people are different does not mean they cannot have a healthy relationship. This chapter is full of stories of how these kids looked past their differences and focused on what they shared in common. These kids have taught me more than I have taught them. They have taught me that love and respect can tear down any wall and soften any heart. Jennifer was shown unconditional love and respect. That was the first time she ever experienced that. But I bet she tells her children about her Teen Leadership class. And I bet her children *will* know unconditional love and respect. With these children, the lemonade business is booming!

Chapter 6

STUDENTS CHANGING TEACHERS' LIVES

Everyone knows teachers do not become teachers for the money. Most teachers I know entered the teaching profession to make a difference in the lives of their students. Every year there are contests asking students to send in nominations for teachers who have made a positive influence on their lives. Very seldom does one hear about students making a major impact on teachers. Yet this is what I love most about Capturing Kids' Hearts conferences. I have seen students time and time again give speeches that have changed teachers' lives. So break out the tissues and enter the stories of these incredible young people. This chapter comes with a warning. Some of the stories will be difficult to read. They were difficult to write. They were even more difficult to experience. Life has handed these students lemons. They not only have made lemonade; they have built a lemonade stand. Teachers who attend these conferences have bought the lemonade and enjoyed every drop.

Capturing Kids' Hearts Conferences

Capturing Kids' Hearts is a three-day training that teaches teachers how to lower the anxiety of their students, build high-performing teams, and provide a safe environment for their kids. Their slogan is "If you have a kid's heart, you have his mind." After two days of the training, the teachers have heard the facilitator tell them how life changing the Capturing Kids' Hearts process can be. While that statement is true, it does not have nearly the impact as the students' speeches. The last hour of the second day, a Teen Leadership teacher will bring six students to tell the teachers how Teen Leadership and the Capturing Kids' Hearts process had changed their lives.

When we arrive at the seminar, the students have a few minutes to meet and greet the teachers during a break. The students know the order in which they will speak. So the students and I sit in seven chairs located at the front of the conference room. There are usually approximately fifty teachers in attendance. Each student gives a three- to five-minute speech. When they are finished, I give a speech describing the Capturing Kids' Hearts process from a teacher's perspective. The students are instructed to talk about our class and some of the most important lessons taught in the class. But the most important part of the speech is the life stories and how the class has made an impact on them.

Isaac

I have always been amazed by the courage the students demonstrate in these CKH conferences. When I was thirteen or fourteen years old, I would not enter a room with fifty teachers, much less give a speech in front of them. Some of the students have been a little more apprehensive than others, however.

Isaac was a shy, introverted student. He always did his work but struggled somewhat socially simply because of his extreme timidity. I felt horrible having to give Isaac, this "A" honor roll student, two zeros on his first two speeches of the semester. When the class was giving their second speech, everyone had spoken except Isaac. I told him he was the last student and needed to give his speech. He continued to stare straight ahead while sitting in his desk. The last time I saw eyes that dark and empty was when I saw *Jaws* back in the '70s. I asked him again, hoping to receive some type of visible response. He responded, but not like I expected. Still facing straight ahead, he covered his face with both hands and began rocking his body forward and backward while moaning loudly. He was simply too afraid to stand up in front of the class. I did not want Isaac to fail his elective class, so I scheduled a conference with Isaac and the school counselor. I was thinking it might be best for Isaac to get his schedule changed to an elective that did not require speeches.

We offered a schedule change to Isaac, and to my great surprise he declined. We told him we would have to do something if he refused to do our next speech.

Well, the next speech rolled around, and Isaac gave his first speech. Granted, it was terrible, but I gave him an A for having the courage to stand up in front of the class. What followed left me astounded. Isaac's second speech was actually good! The next speech was even better and contained a very clever sense of humor. Even though his speeches drastically improved, this does not mean his speeches were void of fear. With each speech, we could visibly see Isaac's knees shaking, yet he overcame his fear. We held to a quote given us at CKH conference by a principal from another district. We would always say, "Never fear the challenge. Always challenge the fear." Isaac challenged his fear and in so doing freed himself from its bondage. Seeing Isaac's transformation was the highlight of my school year. I had to find some way to reward his heroic comeback!

A few weeks later, I received an invitation to another CKH conference. When considering which students I should invite, Isaac's name was the first on the list. The next day, I called Isaac out in the hall to invite him to tell his story at the next CKH. I knew he would decline, but I thought it would encourage him that I asked and that I felt he was capable of speaking in front of so many teachers. Without even hesitating, Isaac accepted!

On the day of the CKH, Isaac was nervous all day at school. We left school at 2:00 p.m. to travel to the conference. I was relieved to see Isaac walk around the corner of the hall to meet us in the lobby. When it was time for the student speeches, Isaac stood to give his speech. I was calm on the outside, but on the inside, I was terrified. I think I was more nervous than Isaac (if that was possible).

I will never forget how Isaac began his speech.

"Mr. Bridges wanted me to come give this speech to you because he said I was … (Isaac paused and gasped such a deep breath that all oxygen left the room) the "scaredest" kid he ever had in any of his classes."

He went on to deliver one of the funniest speeches I ever heard at a CKH. His entire speech was about his battle to overcome his fear. The teachers thought he was exaggerating his fear to make the speech humorous. They had no idea Isaac was simply telling the bare, unadulterated truth. In a way, this made the speech even funnier, especially for me and the other students. We knew what Isaac had to endure to complete the speech. In all my years of teaching, I have never been prouder than I was of Isaac that day. I will never forget him. It was the greatest feat of courage I have witnessed in any of my students. I was even prouder when heard that the extracurricular activity he was most involved in later (in high school) was theater. He excelled, while playing several major roles throughout high school; all of this from a young man who was too shy to answer another student if he or she asked to borrow a pencil.

Hannah

The most challenging portions of any speech are the introduction and conclusion. Teenagers and adults alike struggle with how to start their speeches and how to end their speeches. I cannot remember how many sermons I heard growing up in church when the preacher said, "In conclusion …" and thirty minutes later was still going strong. I have been as guilty as anyone. I once gave a sermon that was so bad I stopped in the middle of it and said, "I have had enough of this. How about you? Let's go eat lunch." The whole congregation laughed. They loved me and supported me, but they also knew it was not one of my shining moments.

In Teen Leadership, we help the students with their introductions and conclusions by encouraging them to memorize both. They do not have to memorize their speech, but they do need to memorize their introduction and conclusion. If the students have a strong introduction, it gives them confidence to finish their speech strong as well. On the same token, one could give a great speech, but if the conclusion is poor, it takes away the impact of the speech as a whole. While I was planting a church several years ago, I had a job selling residential security systems. In the sales training, they taught us the customer would remember the first thing you say and the last thing you say. This also holds true for speeches.

I encourage the students to begin their speech with an "attention getter." It needs to be exciting or it needs to tap into the listeners' curiosity. This gives the audience reason to listen to the rest of the speech. Horror movies have done a great at introducing their movies. The movies begin with eerie music, and it is usually dark. A murderer or monster seemingly comes out of nowhere to terrorize the audience as well as the poor victim. The next scene is the next morning with lovely wildflowers swaying with the breeze accompanied by carousel music. But that does not matter, because the director has already grabbed our attention.

The best attention getter I ever heard at a CKH seminar was by a twelve-year-old seventh grader. Her name was Hannah. She had a bubbly personality and a smile that would light up the room. Yes, in class it was often a challenge encouraging her to stop talking, but I never could be angry with her. It was just Hannah. When I redirected her, she always smiled and apologized and was quiet … at least for a couple of minutes. What impressed me the most about Hannah was how fun loving she was while dealing with some very difficult family circumstances.

At Hannah's CKH, the teachers were seated on the outside of tables which were in a horseshoe shape around the room.

As Hannah stood to give her speech, she approached a table of teachers, her eyes fixed on one particular teacher. "You ruined my life," she said sternly. She then slowly walked to another table. Again, making eye contact with what looked like a seasoned football coach, she said, "You ruined my life!" The coach looked at her with a puzzled look on his face. You could see what he was thinking by observing his facial expression. *Girl, I've never seen you before. How could I have ruined your life?* Hannah then walked across the room and leaned forward with her hands on the table of three more teachers. She singled one out and, as she glared into her eyes, said, "You ruined my life!" The atmosphere in the room was becoming somewhat awkward. It took a tremendous amount of courage for Hannah to continue this introduction with three different teachers. She slowly retreated to the place where she had begun her speech. The tension in the room was palpable, and just when we thought it could not be more uncomfortable, Hannah quietly continued her speech.

"I heard these words come out of Mother's mouth when I was nine years old. What do you do when you are nine years old and the person who is supposed to love you more than anyone else in the world tells you that you ruined her life?" After a slight pause she continued. "I dealt with it by turning to drugs and alcohol when I was ten." The room was completely silent. No one in the room was even moving.

Hannah went on to tell the teachers of her mother's drug and alcohol addiction. She explained how her mother destroyed her own life and then blamed all those closest to her for *making* her turn to the drugs and alcohol. Hannah was convinced for years that her mother was an addict because she was such a bad daughter. She turned to the drugs in an attempt to rid her of the emotional pain she was facing on a daily basis. She did not have the emotional capacity or the tools to deal with the pain in a healthy manner.

Hannah explained how her life changed when she came to our Teen Leadership class. She told the teachers how the class really became a second family to her. She said our sentimental show 'n' tell initiated this family atmosphere. Many kids shared some very difficult things they had been through and over half the class was crying. It helped the students tremendously to know that they were not the only ones going through difficulties. Even as adults, we know that when we go through crises in our lives that it feels like we are the only ones going through it, and the only one who has *ever* gone through it. Of course, we know this is not the case, but that does not eliminate the feelings of despair and isolation. Yet as Hannah's speech continued, one could hear the determination in her voice and the hope in her eyes.

"In Teen Leadership, Mr. Bridges taught me that my mother's decisions were just that: her decisions. I did not cause my mother to do drugs and become an alcoholic. She chose that lifestyle of her own free will. He also showed me that she probably went through a very difficult childhood as well, which may have led to her addictions. I had never thought of that. It actually really helped me forgive my mother. I also learned that I can only control my actions and my attitudes. And when I grow up, I am going to be a great mother to my children!"

I was standing at the back of the room to make sure the kids stayed within the time frame they were given for their speeches. As Hannah spoke, my chest began to swell with pride, not because of anything I had done but because I was so proud of her. Seeing where she was when she came to my class and watching her give a speech that completely mesmerized fifty teachers was almost more than I could take. I thought, *Don't cry. You will mess her up.*

About that time, Hannah turned and looked at me. She began to sob as she concluded her speech. "I want to thank you, Mr. Bridges, for everything you have done for me. You have been like a father to me, and you are my hero. I don't know where I would be today if it wasn't for you." At that point, the floodgates opened, not only for her but also for me. But that was fine. We fit right in with all the other teachers in the room. Hannah received a standing ovation.

In following the schedule for the training, I was supposed to follow Hannah's speech with one of my own. Honestly, I have absolutely no recollection of my speech. I am sure it paled in comparison to Hannah's.

Karen

I first mentioned Karen in the "Perfect Storm" chapter. You read about her story in her own words. It is a tragic story, or at least it would be if not for the positive choices she has made. I could see great potential in her from the first week of school. By the year 2020, Karen will tell others of her childhood and people's jaws will hit the floor. They will be amazed and inspired by how Karen has taken such tragic circumstances growing up and has made such positive strides. I have no doubt Karen will reach her dream of becoming a lawyer. I pity the lawyers across the bench from her.

When I invited Karen to attend the CKH, many students and teachers raised their eyebrows at my decision. Remember I mentioned previously that although these young people have been very courageous and have overcome incredible obstacles in their lives does not mean they are perfect. I often remind the students it is not where they are that is important but where they are going. Karen often says things that remind us all that we are all in process in this journey called "life." Yet her story is important. Her story is inspirational.

Over the last five years, I have brought over one hundred students to twenty CKH conferences. I have seen several students receive standing ovations. Karen was the first student to receive three standing ovations *while she was giving her speech!* Three times, she had to stop and wait for the cheering and applause to come to an end. She spoke about how Teen Leadership helped her stop doing drugs and cutting herself, as well as how to deal with her anger in a positive way. It is interesting how the teachers relate to these kids while they give their speeches. Many of the teachers have overcome similar situations in their own childhoods. Several teachers commented that they were inspired to reach out to their own students who seemed unreachable, much like Karen.

Cherise

One of the most timid students I ever brought to a CKH (besides Isaac, of course) was a girl named Cherise. Cherise was naturally shy, which made speeches a tremendous source of anxiety for her. But this was coupled with the fact that Cherise was an ESL student. Cherise was a very sweet girl and was well liked in the class. At first glance, most teachers would assume Cherise was raised in a "perfect home." There was no way a girl this kind and well behaved could have had a challenging upbringing. Her speech had a tremendous impact on the teachers who heard her speak.

> My mom and dad have supported me and encouraged me to do well in school and reach my goals in life. I could say if it was not for them, I would never have been in Coach Bridges' class. This class has helped me tremendously in my home life. This class has taught me to respect and listen to my parents. It has also taught me to care not only for my parents but for my siblings as well. No matter what I was going through, I could always talk about it in Coach Bridges' class. No one would make fun of me and I could be myself. His class was the only class I did not have to put on a mask. The whole class accepted me for who I was. Many times I left Teen Leadership feeling like this huge weight was lifted off my back.
>
> My dad had become an alcoholic by the time I was seven years old. Ever since then, my eyes have been opened to many things. I remember my dad coming home in the middle of the night yelling and screaming, saying things

I never wanted to hear from my father. As I grew up, my dad's condition grew steadily worse.

People would ask me about my dad and I would tell them my dad was not around anymore. I was ashamed for people to know about my dad. To me, my father was a dead person. Year after year it was like that.

A week before my ninth birthday, my dad did not come home on a Saturday night. To me, that was normal, so I did not think much about it. But after a couple of days and he still had not come home, I wondered if he would ever come home again. I remember the pain of watching my mother cry every night, setting only three plates at the table and the awkward silence at the dinner table. We all knew my dad was not there, but no one ever said anything about it.

I felt like my dad never cared about us in his whole life. I was nine years old, not knowing what to feel or say. I had to be strong for my mom and brother. I needed to let my mom know I was okay. But inside, I felt like a little tiny person screaming at the top of her lungs. I had to look at my brother's sad face and tell him not to worry because Daddy will come home. But I knew it was not going to happen any time soon.

My father became my enemy. I never wanted to see his face or hear what he had to say. But as I got older, I learned to forgive … to love … and to listen. Even though my dad was still not home, I always had the small hope that he would one day come home. And when he did, I would receive him with love and forgiveness.

On Monday morning, a week before my thirteenth birthday, we pulled up the house and saw a man standing on the porch with tears in his eyes. He looked so bad my mother did not recognize him, but I did. I jumped out of the car and ran and jumped in his arms and said, "Welcome home, Daddy." I could not be mad at him. He was my dad and I will always love him no matter what he does.

I forgave my dad, and over time, I learned to respect him in every way. He is important to me. In Teen Leadership, I learned to look at life much differently than I did before. I thank Coach Bridges for helping me realize how important family really is to me. My family and friends see a new "me." And as for my dad, I will never have anger towards him or hold a grudge. Coach Bridges taught me that if I did not forgive my dad, I would only be hurting myself and I respect myself too much to let that happen. Thank you.

After the speeches, we were dismissed to the dining hall where we would have dinner with the teachers. The students and I sat at different tables so we could visit with the teachers and give the teachers an opportunity to sit by the students they would like to get to know better. We finished dinner and left the dining hall to prepare for the two-hour drive back to our school. As soon as we exited the dining hall, all the students sprinted for the school district's Suburban while screaming like it was the last day of school! They were so excited. It was strange how they were magically transformed back into typical middle school students the second they walked outside. I looked around hoping to find the person responsible for these crazy kids.

As I looked around, I noticed one of my students was walking just behind me. It was Cherise. I gave her the biggest smile I could muster and told her how proud I was of her.

She grinned from ear to ear. "I'm really proud of myself too!"

"You should be," I responded.

"No, Coach Bridges, you don't understand. During dinner, three different teachers came up to me and thanked me for my speech. They told me I taught them a lesson today that they should have learned forty years ago!"

Yes, we often hear of how teachers change the lives of their students. Very few times do we hear stories of how the students change the lives of their teachers. Cherise learned a lesson at a very young age that many adults never learn in their lifetime. Cherise learned the power of love, the power of forgiveness. Not only did Cherise's forgiveness change her life and the lives of several teachers, just think of the powerful impact her forgiveness had on her father. No matter what choices he makes in the future, he will never forget the day his beautiful little girl jumped in his arms and said, "Welcome home, Daddy!" Not only did Cherise's forgiveness free herself, it also freed her dad.

The Most Unforgettable CKH

All the CKH trainings I have been involved with have been very special. Each one in its own right has been unique and has changed the lives of students and teachers alike. Yet there was one CKH in December a few years ago that was clearly the greatest of all. The speeches were riveting and the teachers were more than responsive. This was the first CKH where I witnessed each and every student received a standing ovation.

Mona

Mona's story is one of my favorites. Her story is not about her challenging home life or any drug addictions or anything of the sort. Her story is actually all about the Teen Leadership class. Mona is full of life to say the least. She is loud, funny, and from time to time, demonstrated some serious anger issues. Unfortunately, she chose to reveal those issues in the middle of class. All of the girls and most of the boys were afraid of Mona.

While preparing for my classes in August, I was reviewing my new class rosters. I was teaching eighth grade Teen Leadership. The previous year, I taught a seventh grade elective, so I wanted to see if I knew any of my students from the previous year. My heart sank when I saw Mona's name.

Mona had been in my career investigations class the previous semester. It was obvious the previous semester that Mona had some major issues involving men. I have built a reputation for being one of the most welcoming of all the teachers on our campus. I shake hands at the door while wearing my patented smile. Students often comment on how just seeing my smiling face lifted them out of the doldrums and made them smile themselves. That is, for everyone except Mona. The first day I had Mona in my class, I was standing at the door shaking hands. As Mona approached, I said, "Good morning. I am Coach Bridges. What's your name?"

Mona walked through the door as though I was not even there. I did not discover her name until I checked roll.

The next morning, I was shaking hands at the door with my usual smile. "Good morning, Mona! How are you today?" I asked. She completely ignored me. The day produced exactly the same result, as well as the day after that and the day after that. In fact, that one-way exchange repeated itself every day for the entire semester. She never once looked at me, shook my hand, responded, or even gave me a dirty look. If she gave me attitude, at least that would be something. She literally treated me as though I were invisible. I did not know how to respond to her because she gave me nothing to respond to. The last day of school, I even asked her if I could get a handshake since it was the last day of school. Still, she gave me no response. She walked in the room as though I was not even there. If I have not mentioned it before, some students are a joy to teach and some students are challenge. Mona would definitely fall in the challenge category.

Let us just say I did not exactly feel my heart leap in my chest when I saw Mona's name on my new Teen Leadership roster. I convinced myself to start with a clean slate as though we had no history together at all. So the first day of school I saw Mona approaching my room. I smiled, reached out my hand, and said, "Good morning, Mona! How was your summer?" Mona picked up where she left off by ignoring me once again. I had a decision to make. I had to determine if I greeted my students at the door every day because of the positive response I received from them, or did I greet them with a smile and a handshake because it was the right thing to do? I resolved at that moment that I would greet Mona exactly like all the other students in my classes, whether or not I *ever* received a response. I continued to greet her every day.

About three weeks into the new semester, we had our show 'n' tell. We moved the chairs against the wall and sat in the floor in a circle. Well, everyone but Mona.

"Mona, why don't you join the rest of the class over here?" I asked nonchalantly.

"Nah, I'm good."

She was seated adjacent to a bookcase against the front wall of the classroom. On this particular shelf I kept my high school yearbooks. It gave the class a chance to see what I looked like in high school in the '70s. I thought it would give the kids a good laugh and teach the kids not to take themselves so seriously.

At this juncture of the story, I must insert a bit of history as it relates to the story, albeit quite embarrassing to admit. My senior year in high school, I was selected "Most Handsome." This particular year was the first year the student body did not vote. The school had judges who knew no students at the school to select the winner based solely on their senior picture. So I had a very good senior picture, and I also attended a very small private school.

Yet when Mona turned the page and saw my "Most Handsome" picture in the yearbook, none of this history mattered. The students were showing each other what they brought for show 'n' tell when we were rudely interrupted.

With a loud screeching voice, Mona screamed, "What, Most Handsome? You have got to be kidding! Hey, look, everybody. Coach Bridges got Most Handsome. Whoa, that is the funniest thing I ever heard! Coach, you were *uuuuuggggglllllllyyyyyy!* Most Handsome? How about Most Goofy?"

Mona went on and on for a full two minutes. At first, I laughed with everyone else. It seemed like good-humored fun. But then she kept going and as she seemed to be receiving fewer laughs she began to become more disrespectful. I stopped laughing. The smile on my face faded, and finally, the students felt so uncomfortable they started telling Mona to stop. She finally stopped. There was an awkward silence, but I was in no hurry to end it. I wanted them to remember this moment. After a pause, I addressed the class. Mona was still at the bookshelf across the room from the rest of the class.

"I do not want anyone to mistake my lack of response to Mona to mean her comments were appropriate because they were not." I never looked at Mona and did not elaborate any further on my comment. Seconds later the bell rang. The students quietly exited.

The next morning I was shaking hands at the door. The classroom was in a portable building. I looked down the ramp leading to my door and here came Mona. I told myself, "Smile and greet as though nothing happened yesterday." I held out my hand as I greeted Mona. For the first time since I had known Mona, she shook my hand. It almost scared me. I felt like I was feeding a deer by hand. One false move and she might run away. I asked Mona how she was doing.

"I'm fine. Coach, I wanted to say I am sorry about what I did yesterday. I was out of line. I'm really sorry." A tear fell from one of her eyes.

"I forgive you, Mona." She tried to walk into the classroom, but I did not let go of her hand. "Mona, thank you for your apology. You will never know what that means to me." Mona smiled at me for the first time and walked to her seat.

From that day forward, if I was trying to teach and someone was talking, Mona would stand and correct them. "Coach Bridges is talking. You guys need to quit talking and pay attention." No one ever argued with her.

At the CKH, Mona was recalling this story. Her voice began to crack at one point.

> Every man in my life ran out on me and my family. I did not trust men. I figured if I pushed Coach Bridges away from the start, he would not get close enough to hurt me. I figured he would quit greeting me at the door after a week or two, but he didn't. I treated him bad, I mean really bad. But the worse I treated him, the nicer he would be. I didn't know what to do with that. After that day I made fun of him, I realized that he had been nothing but kind to me and I was just being a jerk. He's the best teacher I ever had.

As she walked back to her seat, the teachers rose in applause.

Razzaq

I shared Razzaq's story with you in an earlier chapter. He spoke of how difficult it was for him to move from Jordan to Texas. He had to deal with bullying, teasing, and all that comes with culture shock. Not to mention the fact that he moved to Texas with his father. His mother and siblings were unable to come for another year.

Razzaq told the teachers the first year in Texas he failed almost all his classes. Since being in Teen Leadership, all his grades improved. The lowest grade Razzaq had in all his classes was an 87. Razzaq spoke so articulately the teachers were astonished he had only been speaking English for one year. He was more articulate than many of my students who'd been born in Texas. Razzaq concluded his speech by telling the teachers that he wanted to be a teacher like Coach Bridges when he grew up. I believe Razzaq would make a wonderful teacher.

In the previous chapter, I mentioned that Razzaq and his family were Muslim and Razzaq was asking me about Christianity. So I was somewhat apprehensive when Razzaq told me on the way back to school that his dad was picking him up. I had never personally met his father so was unsure of how this encounter would unfold.

As we were getting out of our vehicle, Razzaq's father exited his car and walked straight toward me. I took a deep breath and extended my hand. Razzaq's father shook my hand as a huge smile came across his face.

"I love you because you love my son. If I can do anything for you, you let me know."

It was a perfect ending to a perfect night.

Amber

Amber also presented a speech that night. She described how Teen Leadership had helped her deal with being molested. The first time she told anyone was during her "Memorable Experience" speech in our class. She shared with the teachers how comfortable she felt in the class. She told me after her speech that she decided to tell the whole class because this was the first place she felt comfortable enough to talk about it.

The teachers were overwhelmed for a couple of reasons. They were shocked that Amber had experienced something so terrible because she was so gracious and happy. They also had difficulty grasping the courage it took for a thirteen-year-old girl to talk about something so personal to a room full of teachers she did not know. Of course, Amber also received a standing ovation.

Following the speeches, the teachers were given an opportunity to thank the students personally for coming and sharing their stories. On the drive back to our school, Amber shared with us that four teachers came to her and thanked her for her courage and openness. They also shared with her that they too had been molested as girls. None of the teachers had ever told anyone. Yet one teacher in particular gave Amber the greatest cause for satisfaction and pride. The teacher told Amber when she was a little girl she was molested by a relative as well. This teacher told Amber she was going to go home, call her mother, and tell her what happened. The teacher was crying as she told Amber. She went on to tell Amber that she was fifty-three years old. She had hidden this terrible secret for forty years. Amber's courage brought freedom to several teachers that day.

Adam

I asked Adam to come to the seminar and share the story of losing his mother to cancer and how the class helped him cope with her loss and move forward. But more than that, the class helped Adam get in touch with his feelings and realize that there is nothing wrong with being an athlete and showing emotion.

Finally, Adam stood to give his speech. He would be the last student speaker of the day.

> Usually a jock like me doesn't show emotion. But I probably will show some today because of what I have to tell you. But before I do, there's something I need to say. (He then turned toward me, sitting behind him.) Coach Bridges, I want to thank you for everything. If it weren't for you, I wouldn't be here. I've never really had a dad before. He has been in jail most of my life. I never had a father, but if I did, I would want him to be you.

As he began to walk toward me, I rose to my feet. This big, muscular young man gave me a bear hug that almost broke my ribs. As we hugged, his back was toward the audience. As I looked around the room, there was not a dry eye in the house, including mine.

Adam continued his speech. He spoke of life with his mother. He told us how wonderful she was and how well she took care of him. When he first found that his mother had cancer, he did not fully understand the seriousness of her condition. Adam then recalled the day he woke up and went into his mother's room. She had passed away. Adam discovered her body. He was only six years old. As he told us this, he began to weep. He retreated to the corner of the room. With his back toward the audience, he began crying uncontrollably. His whole body was shaking. The teachers were looking at me, waiting for me to do something. I waited to see if he could compose himself. I like to give the students an opportunity to recover and complete their speech.

I finally felt like I needed to transition into my speech, as I was to follow Adam. As I stood, Adam turned around and returned to finish his speech. Now as Adam was preparing his speech, he told me about a poem he wrote for his mother after her death. He asked if he could read the poem during his speech. I told him he could read the poem but I wanted to speech to come from the heart. At the conclusion of his speech, I expected him to read the poem he wrote his mother. I was pleasantly surprised when, rather than reading the poem, Adam began reciting it.

Letting you go was the hardest thing we've ever done.
But we know your race is won.
We watched you suffer; we saw your pain,
So we know your leaving was not in vain.
We had you with us for many years,
You laughed and smiled and wiped our tears.
Though hardships and trials came our way,
You were always there saying, "It'll be okay."

Though you are no longer with us,
We still hear your voice
Saying, "Go on with your lives.
You still have a choice."
Our hearts are broken
Yes, this is true.

But someone this wonderful—
God wants them too.

So you go on home 'cause you're the best.
Your time here is done, so now, Mama, rest.

The audience stood spontaneously, clapping, cheering, and crying. I stepped forward to begin my speech. As the teachers were seated, I turned, extended my hand, and said, "Aren't these guys fantastic?" Each one of the students was crying. I spent the five minutes allotted for my speech bragging on the kids and including details of their stories that they were too modest to mention. As the CKH concluded, I had to pinch myself. I could not believe I was being paid to do this.

We only had space for a few of the stories of our experiences with the Capturing Kids' Hearts conferences. As I mentioned earlier, I would have never even considered speaking before fifty schoolteachers. I have seen over one hundred students overcome their fears and present speeches that have literally changed the lives of teachers. As adults, we often tell teenagers they need to listen to us. I believe we could benefit by listening to them. They have much to teach us, if we would take the time to listen.

Chapter 7

WATCH

It was a cold February morning. I just arrived from my coach's office to my classroom. The bell rang for my first class. I noticed the students were all very upset. Several girls were crying while they held each other walking down the hall. I asked them what was wrong.

"Jeff just got stabbed!" they cried.

"What?"

"Yeah, some kid just came up and stabbed Jeff right before the first bell while we were in the lobby."

I went next door and checked with another teacher to verify what the girls had told me. As much as I did not want it to be true, I found that the girls were correct. Another student tried to stab him in the abdomen with a serrated kitchen knife. Luckily, Jeff was wearing a large winter coat. The coat bent the blade of the knife, but Jeff bent over. He thought he was being punched. But when he bent over, the other student stabbed Jeff in the face twice, once just above the eyebrow and once a quarter inch below the eye socket. The administrators did a superb job subduing the assailant and caring for Jeff's medical needs. Jeff almost lost his eye. He was treated and released from a local hospital the same day. His physical wounds were not serious, but who can measure the depth of the emotional and psychological wounds? Jeff was one of my Teen Leadership students.

Security was tightened for the next several weeks and the mood at our school was quite somber to say the least. Yet kids are resilient.

Things seemed to be returning to normal about a month later as spring break approached. Students and teachers alike were looking forward to a week off. The Thursday before spring break, a frightened young man approached me between classes.

"Coach, Coach, there's a fight in the boys' restroom!" There was an eerie fear in the boy's eyes as he told me. The boys' restroom was just around the corner from my room. As I was rushing around the corner, I noticed two or three girls crying. When I arrived at the restroom, one of the assistant principals was escorting two eighth grade boys to the office. He looked over his shoulder and asked if I could keep the boys out of the restroom until the custodial staff could arrive to lock it up.

I entered the restroom to see why they were going to lock the restroom. I could not believe my eyes. Blood was splattered on three of the four walls of the restroom with two or three pools of blood on the floor. The two "boys" that fought weighed close to two hundred pounds, and both were known for their toughness and fighting abilities. I did not know whether to cry or vomit. I was literally sick to my stomach. I had been at this school four years, doing everything I knew to do to change the atmosphere and reputation of our school. In that moment, standing in the boys' restroom, I felt as though I had wasted the last four years of my life. I knew something had to change. I had to do something, but what?

The next day was the last day before spring break. I decided to have an open discussion about the state of affairs at our school.

"If you could describe our school in one word, what would it be?" Each class provided virtually the same answers. Each class took a moment to gather their thoughts, and then the answers began flowing in quick succession. The one-word answers were "stupid," "violent," "sucks," "drama," "horrible," "uptight," etc. The answers went on and on. None of them were positive. The closest thing to a positive answer was "It's where my friends hang out." Of course, this answer was given by a student who never did her schoolwork.

103

All she did was hang out with her friends, so I am not sure that was really a positive response.

A couple of times, I thought about stopping the answers and moving on to more positive issues, but I knew I could not ignore their answers. Part of their frustration was that they felt adults at the school would not listen to them or were not interested in what they had to say. I owed it to them to hear them out, especially since I was the one who opened this can of worms. Furthermore, they had suppressed their feelings and emotions about Jeff's stabbing for over a month. Once I felt that everyone had an opportunity to share, I asked a follow-up question.

After all these negative responses, I asked, "So what are you going to do about it?"

The kids looked at me like I was speaking Mandarin.

"What are you talking about? *We* can't do anything about it!" responded a few of the students, with the rest of the class nodding in agreement.

"Why not?" I asked with an intentionally puzzled look on my face.

"We can't do anything about it because we are just students. This school has always been like this, and it will *never* change."

"Well, it certainly won't with attitudes like that," I declared.

"What do you mean, Coach?" one girl asked. I was waiting for that question. At least I had piqued their interest.

"There was a university study done back in the '90s. This study was to determine the factors that influenced children's decisions as they were growing up. The three dominant factors were parents, teachers, and peers. In kindergarten, parents were the greatest factor, followed closely by teachers, and peers were a distant third. In middle school and through adolescence, the order changed. Peers, by far, were the number one influence on kids' behavior. Teachers and parents had very little influence. In other words, if a parent tells a teenager they have to do something, teenagers will many times go out of their way to not do it or do something else. Here's an example.

How many of you have heard of a teenage girl whose father forbade her to see a certain boy? What does she do?"

Everyone started laughing because they knew the answer. "She sneaks around and sees him anyway," the class answered, almost in unison.

"That's right! She wants to see him even more because her parents told her she could not see him. You see, guys, you have more influence over your peers than you realize. Why do you think they call it 'peer pressure'? You never hear anyone talk about 'parent pressure' or 'teacher pressure.' Your friends listen to you! You have a voice, and your voice needs to be heard.

"Here's what I'm thinking. What if the one hundred Teen Leadership students I currently have in my classes and the one hundred students I had last semester joined forces and resolved to stand with one voice and say, 'We're going to change our school'"?

"That will never work," they said. "They won't listen."

"How do you know they won't listen?" I asked.

"We just know," they retorted.

"Again, *how* do you know?" The students looked at each other, hoping someone had a good answer. But there was no good answer to be had.

I continued. "So what I am hearing from you is that two hundred eighth graders at this school who join together to bring about change to our school could have absolutely no impact or influence on the other two hundred eighth graders."

Some of the stubborn ones said, "Yeah, that's what we are saying."

"Well, answer me this then. How many times in the history of this school have two hundred students banded together to speak with one voice that they are going to change the school?"

"Never?" one of the students mumbled.

"That's right. It has never been done. So how do we know it won't work?"

After much discussion about how we could change the school, we decided that we needed to identify two areas that needed to be addressed first, so we could stay focused. The students concluded that the two places to begin would be to stop the violence and at least greatly reduce the drama (gossip, slander, etc.). I would love to say that everyone was onboard and excited, but that would be far from the truth. For several students, I simply confirmed the fact that their teacher was indeed crazy. At least they desired to continue the discussion after we returned from spring break.

On returning from spring break, I actually conducted lessons on how to stop gossip and fighting at school. In order to teach the students how to prevent fights I felt it was necessary to demonstrate how fights could be prevented. So in each class, I would get two of the largest boys to volunteer for a demonstration. I would have the two boys pretend to be ready to fight. I then asked the smallest boy in the class to come forward.

"What would happen, class, if these two big guys were about to fight and this small kid walked up to them and told them to stop?" Of course, that question received a lot of laughs.

"They would beat him up and stuff him in a locker," one boy replied between chuckles.

"That's right. They would probably stuff him in a locker and then continue their fight." Then I asked ten other students to step forward. I had them come and stand in-between the two boys fighting. "But what if ten students joined together to stop the fight?" The room quieted. Some were beginning to believe we could do it. Yet there were still the skeptics.

"What if one of the guys punched one of the students trying to stop the fight?" a student asked.

"Well, it would hurt a little, but if you did not retaliate, the guy who punched you would be gone. When there is a fight, the first thing the assistant principal does is watch the video from the security cameras. Most of the fights are in the hall and the security cameras would show ten students trying to intervene and stop the fight instead of standing around provoking one. The days of students standing around yelling, 'Fight! Fight! Fight!" with your fist in the air must stop. It must stop now, and it must stop first with the Teen Leadership students.

Another way you could prevent fights is to tell a teacher or administrator when you hear there is going to be a fight. Forget that garbage about 'Snitches get stitches.' Tell someone who has authority to stop it or prevent it. No one has to even know you told someone."

We then talked about how to reduce the gossip and drama. Granted, I told them we would probably never eliminate it, because there were people in the school. But I told them each student and teacher could resolve to be part of the solution rather than the problem. They were curious as to how they could help prevent gossip. So I gave them some examples.

"Say you are talking to a friend and they start speaking negatively about another student. All you have to do is say, 'You know, Sarah isn't here and I don't feel comfortable talking about someone behind their back. So why don't we talk about something else?' Yes, that is extremely awkward, but you will only have to experience that awkwardness with that person once. I guarantee you the next time they have something to gossip about, they will find someone else who is willing to listen to it. They do not want to be called out or embarrassed again. So they won't come to you with any gossip again.

"If you have a friend who is mad at someone else and talks to you about it, there are several things you can do. You could ask if they have talked to this person about the problem. If they haven't, suggest they talk to that person instead of talking to you. You may even offer to accompany them to the other person so the two of them could work it out. People will only gossip to those who are willing to listen to it. Yes, they will probably start gossiping about you, but you can only control what you do. The fewer people who are willing to listen to gossip, the less gossip there will be."

Over the next week, most of the students took ownership of our new project. We did not know what to call it, or how to organize it, but there was definitely a desire on the part of the students to change the school for the better. I have always been a visionary. I love to tell stories and encourage others to dream. So I painted them a word picture.

"Picture yourselves four years from now, seated in a massive coliseum, wearing a cap and gown. It is your graduation day! The principal of the high school speaks, along with the valedictorian and salutatorian. But then the principal gives way for a couple of moments to Ms. Crawford, the middle school principal. Ms. Crawford looks each of you in the eye and thanks you for changing her school. She tells you that our school has never been the same since you decided to make a difference and change the atmosphere and reputation of the school. With tears in her eyes, she tells you she will be eternally grateful for your resolve, your courage, and your passion. She then says, 'You changed our school. Now go out and change the world.'"

As I finished the story, I noticed some of the students were misty-eyed. They were catching the vision. They were actually starting to believe we could do it.

I finally asked them, "What if we try but fall short of our goal? What if we can't eliminate fights in our school? Will we be any worse off than we are now, or will we be better off for standing up for what we believe in? We really have nothing to lose except the violence and drama."

The kids were catching the vision. I cannot say they were all totally convinced we would be successful, but they all agreed it was worth a try. In each class, students asked if we could continue the discussion after spring break. Of course, I agreed.

I knew if we were going to be successful, we would have to communicate our vision to the rest of the school. I spoke with Ms. Crawford, our principal, and she was wonderful. She was completely supportive of all we were trying to do. Any visionary leader will tell you if you fail to communicate your vision at least every twenty-eight days, the people in the organization forget the vision. Vision is something that must be communicated on a regular basis. So Ms. Crawford agreed to have a Teen Leadership student give a word of encouragement every morning during the announcements. We had a different theme for each day of the week:

> Monday: Stop the violence!
> Tuesday: Use appropriate language.
> Wednesday: Confidentiality and ending gossip.
> Thursday: Tolerance—cooperating with those different from you.
> Friday: Excelling in the classroom.

The morning announcements were not going to change the school, but it was definitely a piece of the puzzle. I assigned a student for every day of school for the rest of the school year. The students were asked to write what they were going to say during the announcements and receive approval from Ms. Crawford before the announcement was given. She was very conscientious about proofreading the announcements and she also gave the students some wonderful suggestions on how they could improve their announcements. We could not have done it without her.

Speaking of Ms. Crawford's support of our project, she also allowed us to go into the eighth grade health classes to gain their support. The health students were my Teen Leadership students from the previous semester. So they already knew I was crazy, and they were also familiar with students giving speeches. By the time the students completed their speeches to the health classes, we probably had 80–90 percent support from the students.

The Friday after spring break, we had another family time to discuss any further ideas the students might be entertaining. One of the students asked if we could make and sell T-shirts. I thought that was a wonderful idea! We brainstormed about what logo should be used and what, if anything, should be on the back of the shirt. Our school mascot is a bear. So a young man named Chris, who was one of the shyest students I had, walked up to me while I was at the board writing down ideas and handed me a piece of paper. On this piece a paper was a pencil drawing. It was a picture of a rather menacing bear roaring with claws held high as though ready to attack. Yet this was no ordinary bear. Half of the bear's face was mechanical. There were other places on the bear's shoulders and arms with holes in the fur. Through the holes, similar robotics was seen under the bear's skin. The bear's paws were also mechanical with claws not unlike those belonging to Wolverine of *X-Men* fame. In the top left corner of the drawing were four words in block letters: A Change Is Coming!

The artwork itself was phenomenal! I was so proud of Chris for taking the initiative to draw it. But I wanted to be sure I was not missing any of the hidden meaning he may have included in the logo. I have to admit I was also somewhat concerned about the menacing nature of his bear.

"Chris, I absolutely love the artwork. I had no idea you were such a wonderful artist." After a pause, looking at the logo, I continued. "I am a little concerned about how menacing the bear looks. Could you explain the logo to me so I can have the privilege of understanding everything this picture represents?"

"Sure," he said, with eagerness he never demonstrated when he presented speeches. "The bear obviously represents our school. The fur on the bear represents how our school has been, and the robotics you see coming out under the skin is what our school is becoming. I wrote A Change Is Coming! in the corner because that's what we are hoping to do. We are trying to change our school."

I showed the rest of the class the picture and explained what it represented. The class loved it. From that day forward, we affectionately referred to the bear as "The Terminator Bear." The classes all wanted to use the drawing on our T-shirts. I was excited because I did not want Chris to be disappointed if the other students did not like his drawing. I never saw Chris smile like he did when the other students would compliment him on his drawing.

Once the logo was agreed upon, we turned our attention to what could be placed on the back of the T-shirt. I suggested an acrostic for the back of the shirt.

Then came their next assignment. I took each class, divided them into small groups, and encouraged them to create an acrostic that would describe what we were trying to do. When the assignment was completed, I had twenty-six acrostics written on the whiteboard at the front of the room. I narrowed the list of possibilities down to nine. I then had the students vote on their favorite. It was important that this project be owned and created by the students themselves. It was a close vote, but the winning acrostic was

W – Watch
A – All
T – The
C – Changes
H – Happen

I loved it because it capsulated everything for which we stood. Remember that during our discussions, I told the students the most difficult aspect of this project would not be convincing people we could change the school. The most difficult aspect would be them living in such a way they could say to anyone, "Hide and watch. Watch us change the school." The most common leadership theme I constantly reinforced to my students was the importance of leading by example. They got it! We ordered the shirts, and when all was said and done, we sold almost 150 T-shirts in less than a week!

If this were all we did, it would be a wonderful story. Yet this was only the beginning. The students began taking to heart all we discussed in our class. I began hearing reports of students *stopping* gossip instead of *spreading* it. Each Friday during family time, students would report to the class things they did that week to bring about change. I personally prevented eight fights during the last six weeks of school. I was able to prevent them because students would tell me when and where they were going to occur. It no longer was "cool" to watch a fight.

One day between classes, I was standing at my door and shaking hands. One of my students who was walking past me on the way to another class said to me, "There's about to be a fight around the corner." He said it under his breath. He never looked at me and never even slowed down. I asked one of my students to shake hands at the door for me and I walked around the corner.

Two boys were at a standoff. I approached the boys in a very relaxed fashion. I crossed my arms and leaned back, and with the goofy smile said loudly, "How are you boys doin' today?" The boys looked at me, rolled their eyes, and walked away. The fight never occurred and no one was reprimanded.

A couple of weeks later, I prevented another fight just in time. I was drawn to the famous "Fight! Fight! Fight!" chant from down the hall. As I sent the students involved to their respective classes, I looked around the hall and saw five of my Teen Leadership students participating in the chant. I reminded myself if the vision is not constantly reinforced, the students would lose it. So the next day in my class, I let them have it. I let them know, in no uncertain terms, that the behavior I witnessed the previous day by Teen Leadership students was completely and totally unacceptable. "When you participate in a chant like that instead of preventing the fight, you make us all look bad. It makes us all look like hypocrites."

We never had another problem like that the rest of the school year. In fact, at the end of the year, I asked one of the assistant principals to do some research and see how much the number of fights between spring break and the end of the school year had been reduced from the previous year. The next day, I was told the number of fights had been reduced over 50 percent! We did make a difference. Not only did we make a difference that year, but the following year saw far fewer fights as well. The entire atmosphere of the school had changed.

Our students and faculty have not only felt the degree in which the atmosphere of the school has changed. Teachers and coaches from other schools have noticed it too. While coaching our district track meet in April 2010, one year after the WATCH movement began, we had coaches from four different schools approach our coaching staff to compliment us on how our athletic program and our campus had changed. They told us how they used to have special meetings with their athletes before they visited our school. They were concerned for their students' physical safety and the security of their valuables. While we, as coaches, felt these concerns were unwarranted, this still signifies how our school was perceived. As we all know, perception is reality. Two of the coaches from other schools told us now our school was one of their favorite schools to visit. This change is due, in part, to the coaches and faculty, but most of the credit goes to the students who took pride in their school and recognized the power they had to change their school.

As a coach, I have had athletes who could perform at a very high level but never seemed to reach their potential. One reason for their lack of performance was that they did not know how good they were. They lacked the confidence to take their game to the next level. There are innumerable students who fail to reach their potential in academics and life because they do not understand the power within them to initiate change. Almost a century ago, Henry Ford said, "If you think you can, or you think you can't, you're right." Henry Ford was right! Our school stands a beacon of what can be done when students unite, believe in themselves, and *act* on that belief.

Forget the lemonade stand. These kids built a lemonade factory!

Chapter 8

LESSONS LEARNED

Many students have told me over the years that there is something different about me. They say I am not like the other teachers. I believe that is, at least in part, due to the fact that I treat my students like they were my own children. A perfect example of this is Debbie, who I mentioned in an earlier chapter. When I asked her how her life would be different if she was raised in my home, she responded, "I wouldn't dress like this and I would not have the friends I have." This is why I tell teachers as often as I can that we do not teach subjects; we teach students. Many of these students have lived under the guidance of teachers and parents who have told them, "Don't do what I do. Do what I say." To me, this statement wreaks of hypocrisy. Therefore, it is imperative for us, as teachers (and parents) to look our children in the eye and say, "Do what I do. If you want to be successful in life, follow my example." The greatest obstacle to our children's success is a lack of adult role models in their lives.

In these last two chapters, I would like to share with you lessons I have learned while teaching in public schools in America and having raised three beautiful daughters. These lessons would equally apply to a teacher's classroom or a parent's home. So if you are a teacher, or simply a parent, take these lessons to heart and watch how positively your children respond. Now let us look at ten lessons I have learned that will enhance your own relationship with the significant teenagers in your life, whether they are your students or your children.

1. Relationship is everything. While there are numerous concepts and truths I have learned over the years of teaching in a public school setting, none are more important than building a healthy relationship with my students. We have all heard the saying, "They do not care how much you know until they know how much you care." The reason we have all heard it is because it is true.

The last assignment I give my students each semester is to write me a letter. That is just about all the instructions I give them. When they ask for more direction, I suggest they could tell me what they liked about the class and/or how I could improve the class because I always strive to improve as a teacher. I also tell them they may feel free to write me any personal message regarding how the class has helped them. I repeatedly have students write that I am different from all their other teachers. They say they feel they can talk to me about things they cannot talk about with their other teachers. This is somewhat due to the fact that our Teen Leadership class lends itself to students revealing more of their feelings about life, etc. But it is also because of the relationship we were able to develop over the span of the semester.

While I try to encourage my students on a regular basis, I can also speak some firm words of correction to them. The only reason these students receive these words is because they know I love them and they know I have their best interest at heart. Without this security in the relationship, the students would either dismiss the "hard words" or do just the opposite as a sign of rebellion. Most students do not like being told what to do. I simply ask them questions that will lead them to the answer I hope they discover for themselves.

Usually at some point during the semester, I will have students complain about other classes or teachers. It seems some teenagers are not happy unless they have something about which to complain. This is when I take the opportunity to explain why some teachers seem to hate kids.

"How many of you have ever had a teacher you thought hated you from the very first day of school?" On average, about one-third of the class will raise their hands. At this point, we review the importance of a good first impression. I remind the students it takes twenty positive encounters to offset a bad first impression.

"If it takes twenty positive encounters to offset a bad first impression, what happens if, by rolling your eyes at the teacher or showing some other sign of disrespect, you make a bad first impression on the first day of school? This means it will normally take you a month of good behavior to make up for that first day of school. By then, it is almost report card time, and that is if you behave yourself for a month. What if during the next month you have six more bad days? You may have irreparably damaged your relationship with that teacher before it ever had a chance to grow."

By now, the class becomes awkwardly quiet. It is obvious that some of the students had never thought about it in those terms. But I continue.

"Guys, I don't know any teacher who entered the teaching field because they hate kids." One or more students burst out saying, "My history teacher hates kids!" I then have to clarify, "I said no teacher *enters* the teaching profession because they hate kids. I know there are teachers that hate kids. But they did not start out that way.

Put yourself in a teacher's shoes for a moment. Say you just graduated college. You have your whole life ahead of you. You have known for some time now you did not want squander your life chasing money and buying material things. You want to be a world changer. You can think of no better way to do this than teaching school. After all, it was your awesome (and incredibly handsome) Teen Leadership teacher in eighth grade that changed your life *(this part was definitely tongue in cheek),* and you want to go out and do the same. You lie in bed the night before the first day of school picturing the students coming to your classroom grateful you have chosen to invest your life in them and their futures. They are happy, respectful, and teachable. They all pay attention, learn, and ace the state standardized test in the spring.

Then … reality sets in. You begin the first day standing at your door while shaking hands with your students, welcoming them to your class with a bright smile on your face. The trouble is half of them do not even acknowledge your presence, and most of the ones that do roll their eyes at you as if to say, 'Wipe that silly grin off your face, or I will.' Class begins and the class is rude, loud, and disrespectful. You try to get them under control, but it seems the more you try, the more they rebel. You raise your voice and they get quiet for a moment, until the snickers begin. They are snickering because they already made you crack and it is not even the end of the first day. Now multiply this over a ten-year career. Resentment and bitterness began to settle in near the end of your first year. By the end of ten years, you are convinced that almost all kids are rude and disrespectful and you don't even remember why you wanted to teach in the first place. All you wanted to do is help kids. But it was obvious they did not want, or need, your help."

After a pregnant pause to allow the emotional impact of the story to set in, I ask them a question with a soft voice and slight grin. "Do you see how it is possible for a teacher with great intentions to become bitter?" Most of the students nod slowly. Then I discuss with them the power they have to change the atmosphere of every class they attend and the mood of every teacher.

"I want to give you an assignment. For one week, I want you to enter every class with a smile on your face. Shake the teachers' hands as ask them how their day is going. Then if you feel it is appropriate, ask them if there is anything you can do to help them get ready for the class. Observe the changes you see in your teachers' mood and how they respond to you. You see, you guys have much more power to affect the atmosphere of this school than you realize."

If you are a teacher and you struggle remembering your "why," there is still hope. Your bitterness does not define you as a person.

If you were a bitter person who hated children, you would have never have entered the education system. If you would like help in building a healthy relationship with your students, the other lessons in this chapter may be beneficial to you. If you have no desire to build relationships with your students, may I respectfully recommend you find another profession? Most kids today deal with an overwhelming amount of stress on a daily basis. They do not need to come to school and have a teacher who cares more about their subject matter than the students they are teaching add even more stress.

Each semester in Teen Leadership, I take a straw poll. I ask the students what their grades are like in classes where they have a good relationship with their teacher versus classes where they do not have a good relationship with the teacher. For six years now, almost 100 percent of the students surveyed say they make better grades in the classes where they have a good relationship with the teacher. Students will want to perform and please their teacher if the relationship is there. On the other hand, if the students do not have a good relationship with the teacher, their motivation will usually be lacking.

Robbin and I have been blessed with three incredible daughters. They have been a challenge to raise at times (mostly because they are girls and not because they have been rebellious), but they have always wanted to please us as parents. This is because we have had such a close relationship with them. In the same way, if students love their teachers and want to please them, they will perform better in school. Many teacher workshops are helpful in providing ideas for teachers to use in the classroom. A teacher could become buried alive in the mounds of material involving strategies, techniques, and "tricks of the trade." Yet *nothing* can, or should, replace the value of a teacher having a strong, healthy, appropriate relationship with his or her students.

I once had a Latino student in my class that I must admit I was not excited to have. His name was Eric and his bad reputation preceded him. But rather than write him off like most of his other teachers did throughout his school career, I decided to forget the horror stories

I heard about him and do everything I could to build a relationship with him. Eric was pretty tough and was never one to open up and share his feelings. Yet as time passed, we grew closer and closer. His mother and stepfather were going through some difficulties and sometimes we would talk for a couple of minutes after class. Teachers must learn to be expert "two-minute counselors." Mostly, the students just want someone to listen anyway.

One day Eric told me he was leaving the school. His mother and stepfather decided to get a divorce. I consoled him as best I could. It was obvious he was distraught and was not looking forward to moving at all. His last day with us he stealthily handed me a letter. His letter illustrates the importance of a strong relationship between a teacher and student.

Dear Coach Bridges,

This is my last day here at our school and I just want to tell you that this class really changed me. I was scared (even though I did not show it) because I had no one to talk to and I thought your class would be a big waste of time. But later on I found out that this was the best class I could have been in. It was really worth my time because I could express my feelings about my stepmom and dad, and my mom and step dad getting a divorce. When you talked to me about it, you helped me understand that things may never change between them, so the only thing I could do is change me and get better every day. I believe I have done that. If it was not for people like you in my life, I'd probably still be skipping school to smoke weed. And drugs really messed up my life. But I don't do drugs anymore.

Well, thank you so much for helping me. I feel like you made me a better person. You taught me how to express my feelings to people, and when things are not going well I need to talk to someone about it, and in the end I will understand and feel better about it. Thank you again for helping me express my feelings, for helping me understand things more, and just know you have changed my life. Thank you.

I have three file folders of letters just like Eric's. I keep them in my filing cabinet for safekeeping. Many of them have brought tears to my eyes, including three letters from students who were contemplating suicide before coming to my class, letters about students who used to cut themselves who stopped cutting, and several kids who wrote to tell me they were doing drugs when they first started coming to my class. Many of them said they stopped doing drugs about two weeks after coming to Teen Leadership. On the days I feel like I cannot possibly continue another day, I pull out these letters along with box of tissues and remember why I teach. I say a little prayer and thank God for the opportunity to make a difference in the lives of kids. It is a good life.

2. Behind every student is a story. The first year I taught in a public school I was hired with an emergency teaching certificate. I was in the process of starting a new church and was selling security systems in order to put food on the table so my family did not go hungry. It was actually a small miracle how I was offered the job. That story may be for another book. Let's just say on the first day of school, I was terrified. I had not been in a public school classroom since I was fourteen years old. One day I was selling security systems. The next day I was hired to teach seventh grade Texas history and eighth grade American history. The following day I was seated in an auditorium with about 1,500 teachers for the district convocation meeting. I spent the next several days in seminars and workshops with this nagging question in the back of my mind: how do I do a grade book?

When students would be disrespectful or disruptive, I would raise my voice and/or assign them afterschool detention. I remember wondering what was wrong with these kids. I lived through most of that first year with a low-level frustration that periodically spilled over into anger. Not until I attended a Capturing Kids' Hearts conference did my outlook toward students really change. I began to see past the behavior, which in middle school can be completely unpredictable and can change from day to day or even hour to hour, depending on the student's mood and what life-changing crisis they faced that day.

I would love to say I made immediate changes after my CKH training. Yet while there were some instant changes, learning to control my anger was more of a process. I very rarely exploded, but there were times I would be seething on the inside. Yet as I continued teaching Teen Leadership and listening to the students' stories, I began to see a pattern developing. Every student that angered me due to disruptive behavior or blatant disrespect had an exceptionally difficult home life. Many of the kids' stories have already been documented in earlier chapters, so there is no need to retell the stories here.

As a word of encouragement, however, I would like to encourage all those teachers who feel like you are at the end of your rope or you "just can't take it anymore" to step back and take a deep breath. Take time to actually listen to your students. Show genuine concern for their well-being outside of your classroom. Give those "difficult" students the benefit of the doubt. It has been my experience that once I hear their stories, I realize I would probably be doing the same things they are doing. As Eric confessed in his letter earlier, most misbehavior is due to some fear plaguing the student.

These fears can take on many aspects. Students may be afraid of the unknown. They never have behaved before so they are not sure how teachers or other students would treat them if they began doing what they are supposed to do. Some are afraid of losing friends or being ridiculed by other students. Usually, this is because they have made poor choices regarding who their close friends would be.

Above these fears, however, looms a greater fear that many times paralyzes the students socially and academically. This would be the fear of failure. I know what many of the teachers are thinking right now. *My kids don't fear failure at all. In fact, they have become adept at failing all their classes.* But I am not talking about a fear of failing math, science, or history. They are afraid of failing at life. Most students who fail public school classes do not fail because they are unable to comprehend the material or the assignments. They fail because they do not try or do not do the work at all. Whether they are aware of it or not, there is a reason for this lack of effort.

It will be a waste of time to ask the student why they are not trying (at least in middle school). The answer will always be, "I don't know." While this answer exasperates teachers across the country, they are usually being truthful. They don't know. This is why I spend little time trying to reason with my students. I attended a workshop where the district superintendent of a school district in south Texas said, "There is no problem your middle school student will have that a little reasoning will not make worse."

Many of these students who do not try or *seem* not to care (I believe they all care deep down) are holding out for a reason. It is actually very simple. If they were to give their all to their classes and they still failed the class, then they would consider themselves a failure. Yet if they do not even attempt to pass their classes, then they have a built-in excuse. "I could have passed that class easy. I just didn't care. School is stupid anyway." Thus, they walk through their school careers while saying, "I could have passed if I wanted to." So the logic is "I am not a failure. School just isn't important to me."

If these students let it be known that they were going to give 100 percent of their efforts to succeeding in school and still failed, then there would be no more excuse. They would be "a failure." Yet the sad truth is that if they did give 100 percent, many of them would not only pass, but would be on the "A" honor roll. For this type of success to become a reality, it would require a tremendous amount of parental support. Unfortunately, for many of these kids, the parents have contributed to their poor attitude. This is why it is so important for teachers to believe in their students, even when no one else does. We all need someone who believes in us.

I had a conversation with a boy in my class who had one of these difficult lives. He was telling me how no one had ever cared about him. He spent most of his life in and out of foster homes, none of which were nurturing environments. He was feeling sorry for himself, which was warranted to a degree, but I shared with him that self-pity never brings positive results. I then told the young man to look at me.

When he looked me in the eye, I said, "I need to apologize to you."

"For what?"

"For taking away your most popular excuse."

"What do you mean?"

"I have often heard you say no adults in your life have ever cared about you. Well, when you signed up for my class, all that changed. I do care about you. So now you have to tell everyone you only had one adult in your life who really cared."

He did what he could to maintain a stiff upper lip, yet the lump in his throat was quite visible. It meant something to him to know a man in his life truly cared about his welfare.

Be there for your students. It is as simple as asking them to tell you their story. You might just be amazed at how much they want to tell you. Many are not used to adults listening to anything they have to say.

3. It is amazing what you can learn by listening. This third lesson is a natural progression of the second. I have always had a wonderful relationship with my three daughters. We have had an open relationship with our daughters and enjoyed numerous conversations with them. The conversations took place at the dinner table, the car, and even sitting on the end of their bed before they go to sleep. I naively thought most children had parents who listened to them on a regular basis.

Well, it did not take long for that bubble to burst. Yet I saw the need for the kids to have an adult take the time to listen to them. This was the impetus to begin an activity called "family time."

Periodically, on Friday, I have the students sit on the floor in a circle. I tell them we can talk about whatever they want to talk about. Obviously, there are certain parameters we have to adhere to regarding what is school appropriate. The kids also know if they tell us anything about them being hurt or others being hurt I must report it. I have been quite surprised at how much the kids open up when given the opportunity.

Avail yourself to your students and demonstrate to them your concern for them goes far beyond their grade in your class. When they are convinced you care about them as a person and not just a math student, they just might let you into their world.

4. Kids are resilient. Of all the things I have learned teaching in the public school system, the one that surprised me the most is how resilient kids can be. I am reminded of Monique, who has had six "father figures" in her life and practically no relationship with her biological father. And her mother had attempted suicide twice. She had endured more than any girl should. Yet she had wonderful grades, was a leader in our school, and had a smile that lit up the room. She was determined not to let the shortcomings of her parents stop her from accomplishing her dreams or becoming the woman she wanted to be.

Then there was Adam, whose father had been in prison most of his life. His mother died of cancer when he was six years old. He had worked hard in the classroom and become a high school football star. He could have failed all his classes and given up on life, but he refused. He is like a son to me and is one student I will never forget.

It is odd, but it seems children have an ability to bounce back from crises and turmoil that defies explanation. It is as though they have a God-given capacity to move forward no matter what life brings their way. There is a popular banner in many schools that says, "Attitude is everything." It is popular because it is true. Children seem to have a much better grasp of this concept than do the adults in their lives. Several times over the years, I have asked my students how they have found the strength to keep going in the face of incredible trials. The most common answer is this: "You do what you gotta do."

We as teachers can help our students deal with some very challenging circumstances in their lives. Unfortunately, we do not possess the power or authority to change these circumstances. Therefore, we must spend most of our time talking with our students, not about their circumstances but about their response to their circumstances. In my classroom, I post a PowerPoint slide on my screen with a quote of the day. I post a quote by Scott Hamilton that says, "The only disability in life is a bad attitude." Attitude is everything, especially during adolescence.

Many students are quick to say things like "I can't" or "It's impossible." Whether they are my students or my daughters, I am always quick to correct them. If they say something is impossible, I have them look me in the eyes.

"It is not impossible. It is just difficult. And one thing I love about you is you can do difficult things."

Far too often, with wonderful intentions, many parents cripple their children by acquiescing to anything the child wants. They tell themselves they do it to make up for the challenges the child has faced. If this thought process is carried out to its logical conclusion, one sees that it causes more harm than good. For instance, if a child has had an absent (physically or emotionally) or dominating father, the mother may spoil the child to make up for the wounds the child has suffered. Yet now the child has been raised with polar-opposite ends of dysfunction. The child grows up having no knowledge of healthy boundaries and certainly learns little or nothing about responsibility. Many parents rationalize this behavior by thinking they cannot discipline or correct their children because they love them too much. Actually, the opposite is true. If they loved their children, they would discipline them. More times than not, these parents raise their children in this manner because they are too insecure to have their children question their parenting skills or become angry with them.

Kids are resilient. They can take much more than we as parents, or teachers, think they can. I know because I have witnessed it firsthand with hundreds of my students and my own three daughters. It is this resiliency that leads us to the next lesson.

5. Set your expectations high. Whether it is your children or your students, kids will rise to the level of your expectations. There once was a first-year teacher who received a roster with her new students' names. Beside each name was a number she presumed was their IQ score. She was very excited to be given such an advanced group of students her first year. As gifted as these students were, she was determined to push them to even greater heights. With each challenge, the students rose to the occasion, even exceeding the teacher's expectations. It was not until the end of the semester that she discovered the number next to students' name was their locker number. In reality, she was given the lowest-achieving students in the school. Since she did not know they were "low achievers," she did not treat them as such.

Teaching a speech class definitely comes with its challenges. Ninety-five percent of my students would rather go to the dentist and have their teeth drilled with no anesthetic than give a speech in front of their classmates. Each time a speech is assigned, I must field a handful of objections describing why students cannot present their speeches.

"I can't think o' nothin'."

"I can't come up with an introduction."

"I know what I want to communicate, but I can't put it into words."

"I don't want to do this speech." (Insinuating the subject matter is too personal.)

This last one is the toughest to answer. I know many of my students have been through the most trying of circumstances. The easy thing would be for me to let them off the hook. But this would only teach them that they could use their past as an excuse for not performing in the present. How would that help them be successful?

So I look them in the eye and say, with the most caring and empathetic teacher voice I can muster, "I know talking about this subject will be difficult for you and I am not going to force you to do anything. But I believe if you can find it in yourself to present this speech. You will find it will bring a great deal of healing. Getting it out in the open is half the battle. But if you do not feel you can talk about it at this time, I will allow you to do a different speech. But you are going to give a speech. Okay?"

In eight years of leading students through the Teen Leadership curriculum, I may have had five students refuse to give a speech and take a zero. The students consistently rise to meet the challenge. This is what builds a student's self-esteem—not giving them a "participation" trophy. After all, I am not aware of any participation trophies in the real world.

It will be difficult to raise up a generation of world changers if we do not do everything within our power to equip our students and children to face the "real world." If young people today are going to make a difference in this world, they must give up their right to make excuses. We all know that oil and water don't mix. Neither do lemonade and excuses.

Chapter 9

MORE LESSONS LEARNED

In the previous chapter, we discussed five important lessons or truths that every parent and teacher should know. A wise man once said, "The two greatest gifts a parent can give his or her children are roots and wings." While the first five lessons dealt with developing roots, the five lessons in this chapter will focus on giving our children, as well as our students, wings.

6. No excuses. Benjamin Franklin said, "He who is good at making excuses is seldom good at anything else." I could say that making excuses is unique to this generation, but that would be a lie. Making excuses or transferring blame onto someone else is America's favorite pastime. It is simply our human nature. Taking responsibility for our own actions is a part of our character that is usually developed over a period of time. It is not at all our default setting.

In the creation story in the Bible, Adam and Eve make excuses almost immediately. The serpent tempts Eve to eat of the fruit of the Tree of Knowledge of Good and Evil, which God told them not eat. When God confronted Adam about eating the fruit, he blamed Eve. "This woman you gave me, made me do it." Eve said, "This serpent talked me into it." So from the beginning, we have always made excuses. Yet excuses seldom bring a positive outcome. I have a friend who is a Marine. He told me that in the Marines, if you make a mistake and a commanding officer asks why you did it, the only response is, "Sir, no excuse, sir." Marines are taught that excuses are not to be tolerated, because many of their decisions on the battlefield are a matter of life and death.

While our young people should be encouraged not to make excuses, it is understood that life is dynamic. The unexpected can and will happen from time to time. In dealing with the unexpected, I learned a valuable lesson from the owner of a carpet cleaning company I worked for almost twenty years ago. If we were cleaning the carpet in a client's home and found a stain we could not remove, we were trained to go the client and immediately show them the stain and explain the three or four steps we followed in an attempt to remove the stain. Then we would inform them the stain was set and could not be removed. Our owner told us, "If you tell them ahead of time, it's education. You tell them afterwards, it's an excuse." I have never forgotten those words. Since then, this principle has helped me in much more important matters than a carpet stain.

If our young people can learn the lesson of not making excuses at their age, just think of how much more responsible and successful they will be as adults. Whatever occupation or endeavor they pursue as adults, they will accomplish more and will understand that in the real world, it is results that matter most. Hopefully, it has been obvious reading this book that my students' strong self-esteem is of great value to me. But in this age of "participation trophies" and a "no wrong answers" philosophy, I believe we are setting our children up for a rude awakening when they enter the real world. In the real world, there are winners and losers. The important thing for young people to remember is just because you lose does not make you a loser. Losing simply gives you opportunity to do better and work harder next time. How will our young people learn to take risks if we remove all risk from their lives?

My daughter Amy entered the all-state choir competition for Birdville High School her sophomore year. She advanced through the first two rounds, making all-region choir. She was the only sophomore from her school to make all-region. The following round was all-area. Those who advanced from this audition advanced to the all-state competition. The all-area auditions were difficult for two reasons. The competition was fiercer, and it was the first round the singers had to sight-read. Amy made a few mistakes during the sight-reading and did not even finish the song. She was so embarrassed because she was one of the competitors who were "escorted out." That is *not* a good sign. When talking with Amy later, I asked her what happened. She simply said she did not know how to sight-read very well and just got flustered.

She could have quit and said, "I'm not ever putting myself through that again!" But that is not what she did. She made no excuses. In fact, she made some very bold decisions that were not popular with the theater teacher and several of her friends. She has always been deeply involved in both choir and theater, although choir is her first love. Last year she was in the fall play with the theater department. As she was rehearsing for the play every day, she also had to prepare for the all-state choir competition. Amy opted out of the fall play her junior and senior years so she could concentrate on the all-state choir competition. As a result of her difficult decision and hard work, Amy made first chair all-state alto II her junior and senior years. She has learned Benjamin Franklin's lesson well. She made no excuses but later made all-state.

When my second daughter, Rhema, was in high school, she was the cocaptain of her cheerleading squad. To say it was a trying year would be a gross understatement. She was excited about her senior year, until she received some earth-shattering news. Her cheer coach, whom Rhema adored, was diagnosed with cancer just before school started. Due to her coach's ongoing treatment that year, the responsibility for conducting practice and developing the team's routines fell to Rhema.

The fall of Rhema's senior year went fairly smoothly. While she held up well under the added responsibility, the challenges began as the holidays approached. Just before Christmas break, the squad's top flyer informed the squad that her parents were getting a divorce so she would be moving away and attending another school in the spring. They had already qualified for nationals in North Carolina that would be held in March. This meant they had to train another flyer in less than three months.

The second flyer was very coachable and was coming along nicely. Then three weeks before nationals, she fell while attempting a stunt and crushed her hip socket. They had now lost two flyers, which meant Rhema would have to revise their routine in less than three weeks.

If this were not enough, report cards came out a week before nationals. Rhema then discovered that her cocaptain failed a class and would not be eligible to perform at nationals. The squad had now lost three cheerleaders and Rhema had to revise the routine yet again.

The squad members voted on whether or not they even wanted to attend nationals because of the losses. It was unanimous! They voted to go and give it their best.

They arrived in North Carolina two days before the competition began. During their first practice that evening, Rhema was catching a flyer during one of their stunts. The flyer accidently kicked Rhema in the jaw. She received a slight concussion. Rhema sat out the next day of practices but was determined to compete the following day in the preliminary round.

In the preliminary round, Rhema's squad nailed it! They were so excited. As they were going down the stairs from the platform, one cheerleader fell, spraining her ankle. Rhema carried the injured cheerleader across the arena. The injured cheerleader said she did not think she could perform the next day in the final round. Rhema told her the team had been through too much to quit now. They taped the girl's ankle and performed the next day.

What was their goal? It was to *not* finish last. When the results were in, their squad finished second in the nation! Those girls learned a lesson they will never forget. The proud papa will not forget it either.

7. Lead by example. Not all teaching is done on a whiteboard or a textbook. While it is important to carefully and thoroughly teach our subject content to our students, there are other important lessons we, as teachers, teach our students whether we are aware of it or not. Our very lives teach students far more than our lectures ever will. We teach them lessons about patience (especially in middle school), optimism, character, respect, attitude, overcoming adversity, and other important lessons every day. Depending on the day, the lessons we teach may be life changing or detrimental to our students.

Before we discuss our lives being an example to our students, I would like to address a few specific areas where we can be examples in the classroom (or the living room with our own children, for that matter). Let's begin with a principle that is often overlooked. *Be happy.* Take a straw poll of any public school classroom in America and probably 90 percent of the students would say they do not like school. Most of the students who do like it, like it for reasons other than receiving a quality education. They like it because it is not home and/or they can hang out with their friends at school. Young people today are bombarded with negativity at home, at school, in the media, and even among their friends. They need a daily reminder that no matter how bad their day has been, it could always be worse. This is why I make it a point to be happy every day, whether I *feel* happy or not. This called "choosing your attitude."

I always make sure I am in the hallway, or at my door, between classes with a big cheesy smile on my face. In middle school, a teacher can receive a lot of strange looks from the students. For someone who lacks self-confidence, this can be quite intimidating. So when I start receiving these looks, I get even crazier. I call it "melting the cheese." I often ask kids, "Where's your smile? You got to come to school today. Isn't that great?" I have also been known to blurt out, "Hey, smile! You could be in jail, or the hospital, and you get to come to school and receive an outstanding education!" While I still get eyes rolled at me, the eye roll is almost always followed by a grin.

Secondly, have a *sense of humor.* This can begin with not taking yourself so seriously. We, as teachers or parents, are still human. We make mistakes. If we can learn to laugh at ourselves, it can do wonders in helping children deal with their shortcomings in a fun and positive way.

Let's face it. School is boring for the most part. This is actually one reason I wanted to become a teacher. I was so bored in school it was ridiculous. Many times I thought, *Can this teacher possibly make this any more boring?* But if the students laugh every once in a while, they will have a positive outlook on the class, their relationship with the teacher will improve, and it has been my experience that they make better grades.

Finally, remember to *be excited.* Your class is your baby. No one will be as excited about your baby as you will. If you want to raise your students' enthusiasm, raise your own. Many students have told me over the years the thing they liked most about my class is that I was always happy and excited to be there. While these principles are important for any teacher, or parent, the most important part of leading by example is living a life worthy of our students and children emulating.

Hypocrisy has hit epidemic proportions in our society. Our young people today are bombarded with stories in the media of leaders professing one thing and doing something else. They see it in church, business, education, celebrities, professional sports, and politics. Many young people have become jaded. They have simply come to the conclusion that hypocrisy is "normal." While it is true there is a measure of hypocrisy in all of us, we must not throw up our hands in defeat. This is one of the reasons for the scarcity of heroes today. One girl in my class this semester said she does not look up to anyone anymore. I challenged her on that and she stuck to her guns. I told her I would do everything within my power to change that.

Please permit me here to share anecdotally from personal experience why leading by example is so important to me. I shared earlier in the book that I spent several years in what would be considered full-time church ministry before entering the field of education. Hypocrisy in the church is one reason I chose this new path. The message that I hated to hear preachers say is, "Don't do what I do; do what I say." That sentiment would be wonderful *if it were anywhere in the Bible!* I never said that from any platform. It is my belief that a preacher, politician, educator, or any other leader in society should live their lives in a way they would want people to follow.

Being an example to my students is one of my highest priorities. But before anyone accuses me of walking on water, I would like to state I am not perfect, nor have I ever claimed perfection. But I can say with a clear conscience that I do my best to live my life in way that I could tell my students, "If you want to know how to live a happy successful life, watch me." Those times I fall short, especially in a forum that is witnessed by my students, I confess it and ask them to forgive me. If we expect our students to take responsibility for their actions, we must take responsibility for our actions. Remember kids learn primarily by observation. This is why it pains me when I hear teachers talking among themselves about partying or getting drunk on the weekend. The philosophy is "I won't be around my students," thank goodness. It is sad, however, that many teachers indulge in the very self-destructive practices they encourage their students to avoid. Yet I guess it is easier, when a student asks a teacher if they participate in these activities, to avoid the subject altogether or tell them it is none of their business than for the teacher to change their own behavior.

It is not my intention here to judge teachers. Most teachers I know have a heart for kids and live very wholesome lifestyles. I am just drawing attention to an issue I believe to be vitally important to our youth today. It would be a tragedy for our children to grow up believing happy, healthy, wholesome lives are to be relegated to fairy tales. I want my students to know that "happily ever after" is possible. How can they start believing this could be a reality, if they never see it for themselves? Our children are desperate to see adults who are trustworthy, honest, caring, happy, and successful. This is the kind of life they want to live. It is our responsibility to show them the way.

8. Be a visionary. Beginning with Lewis and Clark, the pioneer spirit in America would be a catalyst for untold number of pioneers to travel west. Some were in search of riches, some simply to begin a new life, and some to satisfy an unquenchable curiosity of what the next frontier held in store for them. To help them prepare for the challenges of the frontier, these pioneers would often send scouts ahead of them so they would know what to expect.

One of the challenges faced by any teacher or parent is motivating teenagers to think long term and consider their future. Most teenagers' idea of long-term planning is what they are going to do this Saturday night. They live in the moment and make decisions based on how they will be affected in the here and now. It is difficult for them to see how daily decisions today will affect them when they are twenty-five or thirty years old. For example, how they treat their parents and teachers will have a direct result on how they will treat their bosses in the real world. Habitual tardiness to class usually results in being habitually late to work later in life.

On the positive side, finishing a project two weeks before it is due could translate into being an employee who is proactive, organized, and thus, very productive. Starting a new club or being student council president may prepare a young person for a successful life as an entrepreneur or a central figure on a management team.

Unfortunately, the only feedback many teenagers receive from their parents, and many times teachers, regarding their future is negative.

"You're never going to amount to anything."
"You are a lazy, good-for-nothing bum."
"You're probably going to end up in jail, or dead, before your twenty-first birthday."

These are quotes my students have shared with me while describing their family talks. As a result, many have given up on having a bright, successful future. After all, if their own parents do not believe in them, why should they believe in themselves?

Whether we are parents, teachers, or simply mentors in the lives of teenagers, we have a responsibility to be visionaries. We need to look for reasons to encourage them. We need to speak to the positive things we see for their future. On a regular basis, I will call a student up to my desk, have them look me in the eye, and speak into their lives.

I had one student who was being raised by two alcoholics. His mother and father fought on a daily basis. They would curse at one another and at him. No matter how hard he tried, he could never please his parents. Despite his home life, he was always positive with his friends and teachers and very well behaved. Although whenever a class discussion would drift toward parents, I noticed Bobby would get very quiet and stop participating in the discussion. Most kids in his situation would be on drugs and a constant problem in the classroom, but not Bobby. One day I called him to my desk for a short conversation.

"Bobby, I am sorry for all the things you have to deal with at home." He was the oldest of four siblings and most of the responsibilities at home parents would be expected to carry were placed on Bobby's shoulders. "Let me ask you a question. Do you know how your mother and father were raised?"

Sadness covered his face like a cloak. "Yes, sir. My mother was sexually abused by her father, and my dad was raised by an alcoholic father who would constantly yell at him and beat him whenever he would mess up. My dad hates his dad so much we are not even allowed to talk about him." There was a quizzical look on Bobby's face, as if he was wondering why I was putting him through this.

"Bobby, before you allow any bitterness to grow in your own heart, keep in mind that your parents were once teenagers trying to deal with very similar issues you are facing today. They have raised you the way they have because it is all they know. It doesn't make your parents bad people. It simply means that *hurt* people hurt people. No one has ever showed them how to be a positive parent. Understand I am not excusing their behavior. I just want to help you see your parents in a little different light.

There is something else I need to tell you though, and I need you to look me in the eye."

Bobby raised his head slowly.

As our eyes made contact I continued. "Bobby, your son will never say the things you have said about your father, or that he has said about his father. In fact, your son is going to tell others how you changed your family history. He is going to tell others how bad your family had been for generations and how you put an end to it. Your son will tell others he has the greatest dad ever, and he will be right."

A tear fell from his eyelashes like a raindrop falling from a leaf after a spring rain. As he wiped away the tear, a smile crossed his face like I had never seen. "Thanks, Coach."

Some readers may be thinking, *That's great for you, David but I am not a visionary.* If this is you, may I encourage you to start by simply encouraging your students. A little encouragement can go a long way toward turning a young person's life around. Just ask some of the following students.

> Hi, my name is Kathi. Self-control, power, and love: these are just a few of the things my life needs. Even after plenty of attempts at fixing my life, I failed. At least this is what I thought until I entered the eighth grade. By the first day of school though, I had enough of my life and I was ready to end it all. Toward the end of the famous first day, I go up to the door of my next class. I see this teacher standing at the door SMILING. I remember wondering what was wrong with him. Little did I know he was about to change my life forever. Then later that month my cutting (yeah, I cut) got worse. I tried to quit but to my expectation, I

failed (again). But much to my surprise, I grew to love the Teen Leadership class taught by the one and only Coach Bridges. He changed my life the most.

Coach Bridges encouraged me, listened to me, and pushed me to quit cutting. I did. And for this he will always be my hero. Wow! I didn't think I would ever have a hero.

What Kathi didn't share in her story is that she had virtually no relationship with her father (sound familiar?) and for a couple of years was homeless, living with her mother on the streets. I did not have any great words of wisdom that convinced her to quit cutting. I just loved her and painted a picture of her future much greater than she ever imagined. Over time, she began to believe that picture and made it her own. She is now in high school and doing extremely well. She has never been happier.

Another student, MacKenzie, wrote me a letter I will keep forever. MacKenzie was always warm and friendly, with a smile that would light up the room. One day while were discussing issues surrounding abuse, I noticed MacKenzie was crying. Later, one of her friends convinced her to tell me about her being abused by her uncle. We made a report to the authorities and she received the help she needed. Her persistence in school and in life, not to mention the courage she demonstrated in coming forward about her abuse, inspired me. I told her she was one of my heroes. She could have turned to drugs or alcohol to deaden the pain she was feeling inside, but she did not allow herself to go there. She kept making the right choices in spite of the challenges all around her.

Coach Bridges,

Wow, where do I start? You started out as my teacher, then my friend, and now, my hero. You have shown me who I really am. I am MacKenzie, the girl that makes people laugh, the girl who has a great personality, and the girl that has a pretty smile and never holds grudges. But through everything, I have noticed that I have people who hate me. But that's okay because I also have people who love me, like you and Jessica (the friend who told her to tell me about the abuse).

But I really wanted to write you because I really appreciate everything you have done for me. Without you, I don't know what I would have done. I am sorry I put you through everything about my uncle, but I chose to pick a person I could totally trust, and that person was you. Thank you so much. You are my hero.

MacKenzie

PS: Tell me how I am your hero, when you're the one that's saving my life.

MacKenzie called me her hero. While I am grateful for her kind words, there was nothing heroic about what I did. All I did was show her I cared and was trustworthy enough for her to tell me about the abuse she endured. I reported the abuse and MacKenzie received the help she needed. I wonder if this does not say more about our society than anything else, that a teacher who shows a student they care is viewed as heroic. Where are all the heroes today?

Young people need adults speaking into their lives. They need to know someone believes in them. They need to know someone they love and respect sees great things in their future. They need teachers who consider their career less of a job and more of a calling. What they need are heroes.

9. Celebrate what you want reproduced. There is a very common trap that snares teachers and parents alike. One falls into this trap when they expend more energy on the students (or children) who are misbehaving than the ones who are responsible and are doing what they are supposed to be doing. My experience in the classroom tells me that in most of my classes, there are only three or four students that cause 95 percent of the problems. So we find ourselves exerting 95 percent of our energy correcting these three students while we neglect the twenty or twenty-five students who are doing the right thing.

All students want attention. They want to know that they matter to someone. They want to be recognized for a job well done. But more than anything, they want attention from those significant adults in their lives. They want to please their parents (and their teachers, for the most part). When there is neglect, however, children may resort to other means of drawing attention. The result is misbehavior. After all, the three kids in the back of the room are constantly messing up, and they get almost all the teacher's attention. When a teacher falls into this trap, the atmosphere of the classroom deteriorates dramatically. The kids come to class in a bad mood and the teacher is thinking, *If I can just get through this class, I'll be fine.*

I must admit one of the things I love about teaching is the challenge of reaching students who are considered unreachable. The fact remains, however, students do not have to be low achieving and disruptive for a teacher to make a difference in their lives. When a teacher recognizes a job well done, it can encourage others to do the same. Of course, care must be taken to avoid the appearance of favoritism, but a teacher would do well to spend most of their time drawing attention to good behavior rather than bad behavior.

One of my students was so successful in school I wondered if I could be of any help to him at all. Zach was the top academic student in the school, student council president, and had received many awards in theater. He was extremely talented and well liked by everyone. He was also one of the smallest students in the school. Being such a successful student, I asked Zach to write down some reflections about his Teen Leadership experience.

When I stepped into that boiling-hot Teen Leadership classroom in August, I wasn't expecting a lot. I'd only taken the class because I needed the speech credit and vaguely remembered the teacher being nice. It now hurts to say this, but I thought I already knew everything I needed to know about this stuff. I was in student council that year and I had recently been to a leadership conference in Washington, DC. So who would have thought that a little classroom in school could help me more than all of that? Not me, but I soon changed my mind ...

From the first day, I realized this class had a lot more to it than I thought! I was immediately greeted by Coach Bridges, who I now believe is the nicest person alive. He made us feel welcome, and the class started to have that homey feel. That first week of school, the class started bonding into a family. This was partly because we had our first "family time." As I am sure you have heard, family time is when we push our desks against the wall and sit in the floor and talk to each other about what is going on in our lives. That week's topic was "one thing we wished we could change about our families." And after that class, we all came out crying and holding each other. We realized we were not all that different from each other. That was when the jocks, the skaters, the nerds, the preps, and all the social cliques came together. From then on, that was the class to look forward to, the class that refreshed you and made you happy. We were home in that class.

But the class would not have existed without the main ingredient, Coach Bridges. His constant energy and joy left you ready for anything. He wasn't just a teacher. He was like a counselor, father figure, and best friend rolled into one. I remember a couple of times in particular when he shut the class down to listen to students' problems. He always had a smile on his face. He always shook hands at the door. He was a great storyteller and would always play cool music between classes. It's good to have someone who's dependable for things like that. He made a difference to so many people. Every day he gave us forty-five minutes of refreshment, laughter, bonding, guidance, and learning. He gave us forty-five minutes of love. Thanks for everything, Coach.

From reading Zach's story, one might get the impression that we never did any work in our class. We actually did a lot of work. His class as a whole probably gave the best speeches of any single class I had. They were at least in the top two. But how many of us who have had a favorite teacher remember the lessons in the curriculum? What we remember is the relationship; we remember the lessons about life that are not found in the curriculum. At the same time, when I think back on the teachers who had a major impact on my life, I realize those classes were "coincidently" the classes in which I made the best grades.

It is time we understand that as teachers we must do more than teach our subject matter. Teaching material is not going to impact students. Teaching students and caring about their lives outside of school will impact students and thus aid in their success in the classroom.

10. Never give up. On October 29, 1941, the British prime minister, Winston Churchill, visited Harrow School, which he had attended as a child. He desired to hear the traditional songs he sang as boy and then address the students. When it was time for him to speak, Churchill stood before the students and said, "Never, ever, ever, ever, ever, ever, ever, give up. Never give up. Never give up. Never give up."

If I could leave teachers with one message, this would be it. *Never give up!* Teaching today is probably more challenging than ever. But this also means the kids need us more than ever (whether they realize it or not). The behavior of students can sometimes be enough to send teachers over the edge. Administrative pressures and standardized tests add even more pressure. There is a reason that over half the teacher in America quit within five years, according to a *Washington Post* research study in 2006. But the reward for those who stay the course is priceless. I once took out a calculator and realized that if I teach until I am sixty-five years old, I will have influenced, to varying degrees, over five thousand students. This does not count those I have coached or other students I have influenced who have never darkened the door of my classroom. Then take into account the spouses of these students who will indirectly be influenced, and then the children of all these students. You get the idea.

I wonder what it will be like to sit in a nursing home in the year 2050 and know that students I taught in 2010 are sitting down with their now grown children and saying, "When I was in middle school, I had a crazy old teacher who taught me something I will never forget …" Yes, you are right. I will probably never hear about it, but I believe it will happen. And I know my life will be well spent.

I know powerful stories of the students themselves lead you to continue reading this book. So I thought it would only be fitting to conclude this chapter with a story. Earlier I told you about Teresa. She was the girl who wrote the letter with the "F" words throughout, which I confiscated during class. She went on to tell me how her parents talk to her like that every day. That type of language was as common as "How was your day?" The last day of school, Teresa discreetly handed me a letter. She later permitted me to include it in this book. This is why I never give up.

Coach Bridges,

You may not know this, but I am more grateful to you than anyone in this world for one reason. No one knew, but I had gotten depressed and everything felt like it was against me. I was going to kill myself. I knew how and when. I really didn't have a reason to be depressed; I just became that way. I hid it well. I was happy and smiling at school when I was around people, but when I was alone, that all changed. I changed.

I hated doing speeches (in your class) because I usually had to talk about my personal life, and I was not going to. I had an extremely rough childhood and it still continues. But for me, it is stress that I shouldn't have. My parents still like to think they are children so I am the "parent" with worries and stress.

So when you told me I was going to be a good parent, I already knew that. I am the one who locks the door, turns out the lights, and cannot go to sleep until I know everyone is safely at rest. I am the mother of my family, whether they know it or not, whether I want to be or not. I have instincts and these instincts are what I am stuck with: parental and protective instincts.

I had much going on for a thirteen-year-old. I became depressed and wanted it all to end. You are the reason I am alive today. You have students that you will always remember. I may not be one of those students, but you will always be in my mind, heart, and prayers.

You may not even remember what you did, but I do. You wrote in my yearbook, "Never give up." Those three words made me realize I wasn't alone. Someone cared about me and someone understood. You noticed I was secretive and very protective of my private life. No one except my two closest friends in the world did that. Those three words that you wrote are the three words that kept me from taking my own life.

The school year is coming to an end. I will miss you and your class so very much. I want to cry at the thought of leaving. You have helped so many kids. I am sorry I couldn't tell you this in person, but I would start crying before I got the first sentence out. You are an amazing person and, what I've heard from your stories, an amazing husband and father as well.

I wish I could have gone to the Capturing Kids' Hearts conference with you, but I could never get up in front of strangers and try to explain something like this. You are different though. You are Coach David Bridges, a man who has helped so many kids, many of whom you don't even know about. I now realize I am NEVER going to give up! And thanks to you, I am never going to even try to think of doing that again. I just wanted to thank you so very much. I am going to miss you.

Sincerely,

Teresa

That year, I wrote in many yearbooks. And yes, I do remember writing, "Never give up," in Teresa's yearbook, and her yearbook was the only one in which I penned those words. I might even say God told me to write those words to her, but we all know God is no longer allowed in school. If you are wondering how I responded when I read her letter, I laid my head on my desk and cried.

FINAL THOUGHTS

Though many of the students' stories contained in this book were very complimentary of me, I want to make it clear that this book is not about me. It is about the outstanding students I have had the privilege to teach over the last several years. While they have not all been the brightest or best behaved, they all shared something in common; they are resolved to face their future with a "whatever it takes" attitude. I am inspired by their tenacity and strength of character. Many have faced more trauma in their short lives than I have in half a century, yet they approach life with an optimism and vigor from which many adults could learn. Thus, the purpose for this book. I felt the stories of these courageous young people were simply too inspirational to keep to ourselves.

Many have asked me why I have attempted to merge teaching with parenting. The reason is twofold. First, we are no longer living in the 1950s. Strong family values are no longer the hallmark of our society. Ignoring the parental void in the lives of so many children today would be ignoring the eight-hundred-pound gorilla in the room. The lack of fathers today has a direct connection to students' performance in the classroom. Today, a teacher needs to be a teacher but also a parent, a mentor, and a confidant. Teaching today is more challenging than ever, but the needs of the students are greater than ever.

Second, it is difficult for me personally to separate my teaching from my parenting. Most of the principles I use in teaching, I learned in parenting my own children. Principles like respect, expectations, and 100 percent effort work equally well whether you are in a classroom or living room. I joke with the girls in the class, having three daughters, and tell them that I must approve all boyfriends. It always gets a good laugh, but it also sends a message. It tells the girls that I care about them as people. Many of them do not have dads to "screen" boyfriends. And my experience has been that even though girls complain about dads scaring their boyfriends, they like the feeling of being protected. Students just want to know their teachers care about them.

I understand that my personality is suited for teaching Teen Leadership. Many of the concepts shared in this book flow out of who I am as a person. So the application of these concepts may look different for each teacher. The key is to be genuine. Students see right through someone who is insincere or a poser. In reality, your personality is irrelevant: everyone can love, and listen, and be an example.

I know of no more noble occupation than a teacher. We, as teachers, are blessed beyond belief. We have an opportunity to make an impact in the lives of children that can last a lifetime. I was inspired to be a teacher by my sixth grade teacher, Ms. Valdevia. I have never forgotten her. I ran into her at a grocery store in 1999. I had not seen her in ten years. She talked to me about becoming a teacher. The rest of the story will have to wait for the next book. A couple of years ago, I reconnected with Ms. Valdevia. She informed me she had cancer. She had a chemotherapy treatment the next day and had just found out her transportation had fallen through. I volunteered to take her. We had a great time catching up. She informed me that she had stage 4 cancer. The doctors did not give her a lot of hope.

As I told her some of the incredible stories of my students, many of which are included in this book, her pride was obvious. Even though I had gray hair of my own, it still felt good to please her. I told her how much she had influenced my life. As a lump welled up in my throat, I told her there are thousands of students whose lives will be changed long after she is gone because of the influence she has had on me. We both cried and held one another. We stayed in contact mainly over the phone for the next several months.

One day I called her and left a message. She did not return my call. After four additional calls, I decided to drive to her house. She had lived alone for the past forty years. No one answered the door. I began to fear the worst. I drove home and sat down at my computer. With my hands shaking, I typed "Caroline Valdevia" in the obituary section of the online *Star-Telegram*. There, I saw her photo. She had passed away two weeks previously. I missed her funeral. I was comforted, however, by knowing I was able to tell her how much she meant to me. I think of her every day as I unlock my classroom door. My students are still benefiting from the life of a teacher they have never met.

To the students, I say be everything you were meant to be. Remember that if your dreams do not scare you, you are not dreaming big enough. Do not let anyone hold you down or distract you from pursuing your dream. Do not waste the untold hours that adults, both parents and teachers, have poured into you. Live without regrets. Be grateful. And remember it is not the days in your life that matter; it is the life in your days.

To the parents, be passionate about parenting. It is the greatest responsibility you will ever have. Enjoy the journey—the joys and the challenges. Live in a way that your children will want to be like you, whether they are two or twenty-two. They need you.

To the teachers, I would simply say, "Never give up." Do not give up on your students, and do not give up on yourself. You have within you the power to change lives and impact future generations. While it is true, you may never receive the accolades or be privileged to see how you have impacted your students, we both know, in our own small way, that we have made a difference.

And no one can take that away from us.

CPSIA information can be obtained at www.ICGtesting.com
Printed in the USA
LVOW13s1058140514

385450LV00003B/5/P